Career Services and Workforce Development Centers for Libraries

Career Services and Workforce Development Centers for Libraries
A Guide

Raymond Pun, Arpine Eloyan, and Michael R. Oppenheim

ROWMAN & LITTLEFIELD
Lanham • Boulder • New York • London

Published by Rowman & Littlefield
An imprint of The Rowman & Littlefield Publishing Group, Inc.
4501 Forbes Boulevard, Suite 200, Lanham, Maryland 20706
www.rowman.com

86-90 Paul Street, London EC2A 4NE

Copyright © 2025 by The Rowman & Littlefield Publishing Group, Inc.

All rights reserved. No part of this book may be reproduced in any form or by any electronic or mechanical means, including information storage and retrieval systems, without written permission from the publisher, except by a reviewer who may quote passages in a review.

British Library Cataloguing in Publication Information Available

Library of Congress Cataloging-in-Publication Data Available

ISBN 978-1-5381-8650-3 (cloth: alk. paper)
ISBN 978-1-5381-8651-0 (pbk.: alk. paper)
ISBN 978-1-5381-8652-7 (electronic)

∞™ The paper used in this publication meets the minimum requirements of American National Standard for Information Sciences—Permanence of Paper for Printed Library Materials, ANSI/NISO Z39.48-1992.

Contents

Acknowledgments		vii
Introduction		ix
Chapter 1:	Career Services and Job Centers in Libraries	1
	An Interview with Marzena Ermler	29
	An Interview with Lateka Grays	31
	An Interview with Elizabeth Joseph	33
Chapter 2:	Specialized Career Services in Libraries	39
	An Interview with Kara Van Abel	73
	An Interview with Monika Chavez	75
	An Interview with Rebecca Hastie	77
Chapter 3:	Workforce Development and Impact on Libraries	85
	An Interview with Lori Fisher	99
	An Interview with Megan Janicki	102
	An Interview with Dr. Corinthia Price	105
Chapter 4:	Resources and Training	115
Chapter 5:	Vignettes and Scenarios	131
Appendix A: Survey		137
Appendix B: Interviews/Focus Groups		139
Appendix C: Practice Questions in Interviews		141
Appendix D: Resume Formatting		143
Appendix E: Assessment Meeting with a Job Seeker		145
Index		147
About the Authors		151

Acknowledgments

This book would not have been possible without the help of many people involved.

Special thanks to Monnee Tong and Hiromi Kubo for providing preliminary feedback on the book proposal in the beginning stages. Thank you to Kristine Garcia for offering responses related to career online and Maegan Profeta for the digital photography workshop. Thanks to Mandy Nasr for fostering the connection.

Thanks Marzena Ermler for providing responses to our questions. Thanks to Elliot Felix for speaking to Ray about his work. Thanks to Edward Junhao Lim, Carmen Lei, Frans Albrillo, and Jamie Lin for their resources and support. Thanks to Jody Burum. We think about 2017, and now this is possible! Thanks to the communities of Special Libraries Association, California Library Association, Public Library Association, Association of College and Research Libraries, and BRASS for providing great resources. Thanks to Dr. Merith Weisman for helping out with Chicago style formatting! We like to thank the following folks for feedback and information: Fred Gitner and Berkley Semple from Queens Public Library, Moon Kim for adding Merlot as a learning resource, and Viktor Sjöberg for answering a series of questions regarding public librarianship.

Thanks to Marzena Ermler, Lateka Grays, Lori Fisher, Marijke Visser, Elizabeth Joseph, Megan Janicki, Rebecca Hastie, Dr. Corinthia Price, Monika Chavez, and Kara R. Van Abel for sharing their experiences and thoughts on this topic in interviews; Dr. Taffany Lim for offering resources and answering questions regarding people who are formerly incarcerated; and Seema Rampersad for support and interest. We also like to thank Brooks Rainwater and the Urban Library Council for doing important work in promoting workforce development and entrepreneurship.

Thanks to the Redwood City Public Library for offering a library space where Ray could work and give ample time to reflect on these experiences. Of course, we offer our major thanks to R&L acquisitions editor Erinn Slanina for providing timely updates and feedback for this project and for reviewing chapter drafts ahead of time! Erinn's support has been amazing and very welcomed!

Introduction

Since the emergence of COVID-19, there have been rapid disruptions across industries, forcing every sector to pivot and to adjust to new ways of conducting business and face-to-face interactions. As many as a third of U.S. workers under forty considered changing careers during the pandemic, as reported by Heather Long and Scott Clement in the *Washington Post* on August 16, 2021.[1] In 2020, 4.3 million people resigned from their jobs, according to the Bureau of Labor Statistics. COVID-19 offered a critical moment to reflect on one's current job situation and to consider new possibilities and options. We are living in a time where there are "quiet-quitting," "rage-quitting," and "loud-quitting" behaviors; employees are dissatisfied with their work, open to new opportunities, and perhaps not sure that what they are doing is meaningful to them. Another challenge has been the rise of artificial intelligence (AI) tools and how these tools have been viewed as means for replacing workers, especially in the tech field.[2] Opportunities to reframe, reflect, and pivot their career choices are possible, but how do workers make such connections? One way is through libraries.

Libraries have also been greatly impacted by COVID-19, with increasing and accelerated demands for access to digital content and virtual engagement to minimize in-person engagement as the virus has persisted. Many library workers were also furloughed, laid off, and terminated due to budget cuts. As such, patrons sought support from libraries. Services for in-person activities were transformed into virtual engagements, and now there are both virtual and in-person options for people to engage in such services.

Major urban public libraries, such as the New York Public Library (NYPL), offered and still offer career services such as counseling and resume/cover letter support through virtual platforms such as Skype or Zoom.[3] The Los Angeles Public Library (LAPL) offered virtual programming related to career opportunities, especially for teens.[4] Academic libraries have continued to support their users by offering more virtual research consultations and support for their remote learners. Like public libraries, academic libraries also loaned out hotspots and other technologies to support users who may not have access to such resources.

Today, patrons continue to seek services from libraries to support their career opportunities. Furthermore, libraries can play a major role in supporting workforce development as a community hub. The 2022 survey by the Public Library Association (PLA), "2022 Public Library Services for Strong Communities Survey," collected responses from 1,167 libraries for a response and found

> 60.3% of libraries report economic development and job seeker support as a community need say they plan to address, and 20.7% say they plan to address it in the future. Job and career services are offered as formal (9.1%) and informal (58.1%) support services, or both (10.3%). 23.8% of libraries have specific workforce development programs.[5]

Are you a library worker looking to support and grow the career services needs of your users? This book highlights various case studies and profiles of library workers engaging in such work. It discusses opportunities to reimagine career services for your users and communities impacted by the pandemic. We create a series of design thinking approaches for you to plan your setup and lesson plans to build your engagement with users. We also examine workforce development trends and policies for future planning, both within the United States and globally. These patterns suggest the kinds of programming and services that libraries may consider offering. Throughout the book, we use the term "library workers" broadly to encompass both classifications of librarians and staff who work in libraries of any type. Library staff may also include career counselors, analysts, and support staff who may not hold an MLS or the title of librarian.

The book is organized into five chapters; each highlights specific areas and resources for consideration:

- Chapter 1 (Career Services and Job Centers in Libraries) explores the impact of COVID-19 on libraries and institutions providing career services and offers a basic setup for creating career services and consultative programs in your organization. We also examine positions and responsibilities in libraries that support career services and workforce development.
- Chapter 2 (Specialized Career Services in Libraries) examines specialized career services within public and academic libraries. Highlighting case studies and interview profiles, Chapters 1 and 2 provide readers from such backgrounds with information on setting up career services as a starting point in developing partnerships, collaborative services,

resources, and programming, to support users in such institutions. Readers can apply these services to different types of libraries, but the audience may vary.
- Chapter 3 (Workforce Development and Impact on Libraries) identifies and analyzes the workforce trends and reports, signaling the evolving skills and practices employers may seek and how libraries can identify opportunities to enhance services to meet such needs. Of course, not all strategies are applicable, but the data provide starting points to reimagine various services that can meet users' needs in future job growth and opportunities. We also explore workforce advocacy and policy work that libraries can do to promote community awareness, especially with local, state, and federal constituents.
- Chapter 4 (Resources and Training) identifies and describes resources that may be helpful for readers interested in specific services within career services and counseling for their libraries, particularly business research resources. We offer comments and notes on these resources and creative ways to integrate them into your services.
- Chapter 5 (Vignettes and Scenarios) offers frequently asked questions and scenarios in supporting job seekers in your library. This section is meant to be a reference if you need a quick look-up on how to identify resources for specific community members. These questions, vignettes, and scenarios came from librarians who support workforce programs.

We also include interviews featuring librarians who have provided support for career development and readiness. This book aims to introduce career and workforce development services and opportunities for your libraries in support of your community users. This book is specifically focused on adults (age eighteen plus) and how libraries (academic/public) can meet their career needs. If you are interested in engaging with teenagers, consider reading *Career Programming for Today's Teens* (2019) by Amy Wyckoff and Marie Harris for ideas on engaging with this younger group.[6]

While most of the research, resources, and services described in this book may be helpful, the library must take proactive steps to apply them to their work functions. We cover advocacy work as well. This area is relatively new, and libraries, especially public ones, struggle to maintain consistent funding yearly. Workforce programs, centers, and libraries are a major initiative to promote the library's impact on communities, and stakeholders with such funding will find our work relevant to their community support interest. We hope that you will find this book full of inspiring stories, examples, and perspectives to help prepare you or to enhance your current services and resources supporting career services and workforce development.

NOTES

1. Long, Heather, and Scott Clement. "Nearly a Third of U.S. Workers Under 40 Considered Changing Careers During the Pandemic." Washington Post, August 16, 2021. https://www.washingtonpost.com/business/2021/08/16/us-workers-want-career-change/.
2. Vallance, Chris. "AI Could Replace Equivalent of 300 Million Jobs—Report." BBC News, March 28, 2023. https://www.bbc.com/news/technology-65102150.
3. "The New York Public Library: Career & Resilience Coaching." Accessed at https://www.nypl.org/education/adults/career-employment/virtual/resilience.
4. Library Foundation of Los Angeles. "Winter 2021 News and Calendar." Accessed at https://lfla.org/wp-content/uploads/Final_Winter2021.pdf.
5. Public Library Association. *Public Library Services for Strong Communities Report: Results from the 2022 PLA Annual Survey.* Chicago: Public Library Association, 2023, p. 10.
6. Wyckoff, Amy, and Maria Harris. *Career Programming for Today's Teens: Exploring Nontraditional and Vocational Alternatives.* Chicago: ALA Editions, 2019.

1

Career Services and Job Centers in Libraries

This chapter covers the following:

- Types of general workshops and services offered; marketing and assessment of programs and services
- Collection development and databases supporting career services and job centers in libraries
- Job advertisements for career services, job centers and workforce development support libraries

Libraries are often viewed as service centers, providing and enabling access to information and resources, teaching how to access such resources, and fostering connections between resources and users for various purposes. This type of work suits libraries to build into career services work and support a growing and changing workforce.

In higher education, career services or career development centers, usually located within the student affairs unit, is a department that provides services in supporting students in the development of specific career skills, goals, and options or receiving guidance and support. Career decision-making is identifying future career paths and selecting a major that best supports those goals. In addition, workshops generally support students in developing their skills, such as interviews and reviewing resumes, curriculum vitae (CV), and cover letters. All these resources and support services can be collaboratively built into the library (if you work in an academic library) or incorporated into your services if you are in a public library.

BrightSpot's Elliot Felix and Amanda Wirth Lorenzo cited Wiley State of the Student Report 2022 and found that "only 46% of students feel well-prepared for future careers."[1] Increasingly, these careers will require skills in a hybrid environment. Gallup's Future of Hybrid Work reported "53% of employees expect to work hybrid while 24% expect to be exclusively remote."[2] Remote work is trending despite the need to bring people back to the office. Jobs also require specific skills that colleges may not prepare students for future employers.

According to a report by the National Public Radio (NPR) in September 2022, "workers are constantly changing jobs and getting raises and still struggling financially."[3] In addition, ACT, the nonprofit organization that administers the college readiness exam, issued a report in June 2023 and found that

> of the high school seniors surveyed, more than four in 10 (42%) reported that the pandemic affected their thoughts on at least one college- or career-related choice, and one-third (33%) of students changed their thoughts on two or more college- or career-related choices, (especially those from lower-income or underrepresented backgrounds).[4]

It was evident that COVID impacted students' career choices, especially in healthcare, medicine, and education. "Students were aware that the professionals in these fields experienced high-stress situations and difficult working conditions."[5] There is an opportunity to recognize this development that is happening in society.

This part of the chapter centers on how to prepare those aiming to secure a job or to change jobs. In this chapter, we will explore general practices and programming for you to consider implementing for your community of users.

GENERAL PRACTICES AND SERVICES

Resume and Curriculum Vitae (CV) Writing and Reviewing Workshops—Holding resume-building workshops one-on-one, in groups, or in a class is possible. These sessions can be held remotely or in person. If you are unsure where to begin teaching, here are some considerations:

Resumes can be organized functionally or chronologically. The functional resume is organized based on relevant skill sets catered to the position. This format is recommended for those who have extensive work experience. The chronological resume is organized in a chronological order—all work duties with the most recent appearing at the top. This format is recommended for those with growing experiences and/or recent graduates. In addition, there are templates within Google Docs or Microsoft Word that job seekers can use to complete their resumes. A resume one to two pages long would be sufficient for users to complete (see appendix D on resume formatting as a sample).

CVs are a bit different. A CV is a complete history of one's education, work history, research interests, teaching experiences, presentations, publications, community service/volunteering, and skills set. Writing it requires a bit more time than a resume does. Generally, a CV is required for those interested in returning to school, academia/higher education work, or academic work-related areas. CV templates are available at Indeed.com or graduate school websites. There is no page limit, but two to five pages generally would be sufficient. Users may want to select relevant skills, experiences, and research interests catering to the position. Libraries can offer resume/CV writing workshops, and instructors can review drafts or help set up a template for job seekers to follow. Hour-long workshops can be scheduled weekly; these can be run by interested volunteers.

Navigating Work Systems to Apply for the Job Online—Submitting a job application can be daunting. Sometimes it is as easy as sending a file of your resume and cover letter to an email address, and sometimes it can be as complicated as a federal job system. There are many different systems used for one-on-one industries. Interfolio (https://www.interfolio.com/) is a portfolio management system for higher education. Such systems can be convoluted and confounding to navigate; you may consider offering instructional sessions. However, it is appropriate for the user to have all their information together and submit it at the end. There can be questions that you may not be able to answer, including those concerning salaries or the disclosure of disabilities. An instructional session should boost your users' confidence in navigating these systems online, particularly for those who may not be comfortable applying for jobs online.

Coaching and Consultation—Many libraries offer career counseling, coaching, and consulting services. Sometimes they are hosted by the library worker themselves, or these services may be provided by volunteers. These services can be offered remotely or in person. Sessions can range from thirty minutes to one hour per user. The important aspect of this service is to learn more about your user's career goals. Sometimes, they may not have any idea of what they want to do; the session can be helpful in identifying what their interests are, what job possibilities may exist, and how to work to achieve them. A session will not be able to resolve all career goal questions, but it can provide a head start on finding answers. When you recruit volunteers, they can specialize in different fields based on their backgrounds. This work can help match the user's interest with a career coach in a similar field. Use the Assessment Meeting with a Job Seeker Form to give to job seekers (see appendix E for an assessment form).

Career/Internship Fairs in Libraries—A career/job fair hosted by your library can draw much attention from both job seekers and employers. It is an opportunity to share different work opportunities available with your community. Preparing, planning, and executing the program takes time, as any event does. You will want to recruit employers willing to table their events. You will also want to ensure that you have space in your library to hold such an event. The event could be outdoors or indoors.

Monnee Tong from San Diego Public Library (SDPL) mentioned the importance of library partnerships to hold a successful job fair at the library.

In SDPL's case in 2019, they partnered with Think Dignity and Workforce Partnership to host a job fair for unhoused patrons, and these organizations offered resume and cover letter workshops to patrons during the week prior to the event. For the job fair, the library obtained funds from Councilmember Chris Cate to offer lunch, neckties, handbags, clothing racks, and makeup and hair supplies. SDPL surveyed participants who gave positive feedback about their experiences too. SDPL marketed this event widely to the media, and participants were also interviewed by the local news about their experiences. In the future, SDPL hopes to offer more workshops at the event.

Career fairs can also be held remotely, if you can support the technology for users attending remotely. These virtual career fairs expect participants to have technologies and a stable Internet to access the event. It is still dependent on employers who are available but the good news is that everyone benefits since it is virtual, considering that location can be a barrier to in-person activities. Virtual fairs might provide more personalized information regarding job seekers and their needs. For example, job seekers might register in advance and share their job interests. Recruiters can add and share multimedia resources like videos to talk about their organizations and positions in virtual platforms. Like any event, registered attendees may not show up so it is another risk to consider.

If you may not have adequate event space in your library, then consider partnering with another group, such as a school or an institution that can provide the needed space or a facility. The library can sponsor or co-sponsor the event, as event spaces may have rental fees. After securing an appropriate space for a specific date/time for the event, it is important to connect with employers who are hiring positions or offering internship/apprenticeship opportunities. This requires a commitment to outreach and engagement with different businesses. To learn more about hosting a job fair and its logistics, consult "How to Organize a Successful Job Fair" by Meier (2018).[6] Consider hosting a preview session so that attendees can learn more about the companies and job opportunities and better prepare for engagement on the event day.

Career Talk Series—The talk series can be organized in person or virtually. Usually, experts in the field can talk about the job opportunities in the XYZ field. Speakers can come from various booming industries, such as healthcare, information technology, human resources, and education, to discuss job context and role.

Why host speakers? Librarians Amy Wyckoff and Marie Harris explain why meeting with professionals might be helpful for teens but the rationale also applies to adults:

- Provide an insider's view of the profession or a specific company or organization.
- Reveal information on what education, certifications, or job training are required to enter the field as well as what skills may be useful for success.

- Broaden their view of the career by presenting jobs that they may not have considered previously.
- Allow for an understanding of what employers are looking for, which help when applying for and interviewing for jobs.
- Help form relationships with people already working in the field, which could lead to mentoring opportunities.[7]

If you would like to vet your speakers, consider meeting with them before formally inviting them for a presentation and asking them for presentation slides or past work. You might want to offer a small honorarium, or a gift card, or at least provide refreshment in the program.

If you are thinking of crowdsourcing this series from your community, consider opening up your library space. Springfield-Greene County Library District, Springfield, Missouri, offered a "book speaker" page, where the program can utilize the library's space. The library shared the site as "Let the Library Provide a Program for Your Next Group Meeting" and "Choose from the Library's wide variety of topics."

Minding your business at the library:

- Learn about the library's business specialists, research you can use, online products, and trends affecting you
- Company research
- Demographics
- Economic indicators
- Legal forms
- Business websites and articles
- Managing your money
- Starting and managing a business[8]

The important aspect of this type of program is learning about and collaborating with your local Chamber of Commerce, an association of business firms and companies in various trades and industries, or such trade associations as the American Marketing Association, American Nurses Association, and so forth. You can find a list of trade associations through the national or international trade association directories.

You can also search for associations online, via Google, using the following techniques and examples:

- site:*.org and nursing association
- site:help engineers association

If the talks are held remotely, you can engage speakers across the country and not be limited to your local community. These sessions can be viewed as webinars recorded for those who may be unable to attend. In 2023, California Labor and Workforce Development Agency, in partnership with the California State Library, offered a series of webinars featuring experts from state and local agencies to talk about different careers for the "CAreer Pathways" program, which featured job talks on healthcare, care economy, climate, agriculture, and infrastructure jobs. This kind of series can promote local jobs and center the library's work on workforce development and trends.

For planning any virtual event, it is best to prepare ahead of time. In 2023, the Association of College and Research Libraries' Instruction Section's Virtual Engagement Committee created a Best Practices for Hosting Virtual Events that may be worth exploring.[9]

Skill-Building Workshop—Your library may already be offering skill-building workshops. These workshops can include some of the topics already mentioned, such as job interviews, cover letter writing, resume writing, and technology skills. You may want to survey your community members for what kinds of needs they are looking for as well as employers hiring to promote these skills. The skill-building workshops can focus on specific industries in your community. If you are looking for experts to lead a skill-building workshop, consider your colleagues along with community members or volunteers. Survey your library colleagues and community members to find out what skills they have and would like to share. Teaching others is the best way to learn. These skills can range from doing digital photography to using spreadsheets to general business research. We will cover these in chapter 2, but this is an important area to continue building and promoting. These offerings can be held virtually or in person, depending on the topic.

Human Library—For libraries interested in creative engagement with local communities, consider hosting a Human Library event. These events encourage users to "borrow" human beings serving as open books and conversations. "The aim of the Human Library is to foster conversations that can challenge stereotypes and prejudices. You will learn to un-judge someone, ask questions and talk to someone you may not have the opportunity to meet otherwise."[10] You can organize one based on different job opportunities to ensure that there are ways for users to learn more about the job and work. The Redwood City Public Library, Stony Brook Libraries, and Georgetown University Library in Qatar offered this event to engage with community members on a variety of topics. Read more at https://humanlibrary.org/

Headshot Session—Not everyone can afford to have a professional headshot. In fact, there are benefits for users to have their own headshots, which can be added to their professional websites and social media channels, LinkedIn page, and what employers/clients might see. The City of Camarillo Public Library hosted Digital Headshots events in 2022, "Enhance your professional portfolio" with a professional headshot courtesy of the Russell Fischer Business Collection (RFBC).

Maegan Profeta, Business Services Coordinator, RFBC, at Camarillo (California) Public Library shared in an email in July 2023 about this program:

> I can't claim to be the first to facilitate a library program giving free digital headshots to patrons, but I am someone who understands its usefulness. Every professional needs a digital headshot whether it be for their online profile, company avatar, or presentation icon. Since photography can be expensive and taking your own photo usually leads to a less than polished look, getting a free digital headshot is a valuable professional resource.
>
> I borrowed the headshot idea for a program for the Russell Fischer Business Collection (RFBC) at the Camarillo Public Library. The goal of the RFBC is to help our local business and professional community through the library's resources. The library had the space that the community is comfortable and familiar with, and the RFBC had the funds for a local photographer. Add some marketing and you have yourself an easy and helpful business program.
>
> On the day of the event, I saw the diversity of our community's workforce, this included: two young brothers who were early in their careers, a few writers who happened to be seniors, a middle-aged professional on his lunch break, some savvy library staff, and a mother pushing a stroller with her three young children in tow. This program made a difference to them, to our community. It helped them create a more professional online appearance, which may help their job prospects or networking connections, which can improve their lives, our community, and our local economy.

"Small business employees, entrepreneurs, job seekers, and anyone else with an online profile are welcome to participate in this first come, first served event. Photography will be provided by Ventura County's Motiocanotography."[11] This headshot can be offered at a career fair in your library. You may want to seek a local photographer and/or if a library staff has a talent for taking photos, they may be able to work on this task. Another example: the Tennessee State University Career Development Center organized and promoted "Iris Booth, an innovative, self-serve professional photo booth that allows students, faculty, and staff to take headshots." It is described as an important effort in preparing students for careers.[12]

Interview Preparation Workshops—A key component of a library's career service program is offering interview preparation workshops, which can be held remotely or in person.

Unfortunately, job searching and interviewing can be dreadful experiences and processes. Emily Stewart from Vox described in a 2023 article that companies are seemingly coming up with new, higher, and harder hoops to jump through at every turn. That translates to endless rounds of interviews, various arbitrary tests, and complex exercises and presentations that entail hours of work and prep. There can be good reasons for firms to do this—they really want to make sure they get the right person, and they're trying to reduce biases—but it's hard not to feel like it can just be too much.[13]

This can completely exhaust applicants in the process.

For libraries, there are many suggestions for preparing for an interview, depending on the job. The most important part to consider is to offer such services, have the questions ready in advance (usually general questions), and work with your users who would like feedback. Preparing for an interview can be very challenging, but if there is an opportunity to prepare ahead of time, it will greatly increase the candidates' presence and employability. One strategy is to share the STAR method, which stands for Situation, Task, Action, and Result when given a question and how an interviewee can succinctly answer the question in this structure.

These sessions can be hosted by a library employee or by volunteers. Other aspects of this topic may include how to discuss negotiations and recognizing benefits and red flags in the positions. Community volunteers may be able to offer suggestions to those preparing for an interview or lead a workshop on salary negotiations or identifying red flags in positions during the interview. Red flags can be a myriad of concerns and questions to consider about the position, team, or organization itself. Also, consider hosting sessions researching the industry, organization, or position itself. This will be covered more in-depth in specialized career services (see appendix C for sample questions to ask).

Some users may need a space for remote interviews; your library may want to set up interview booths or small rooms, which can be reserved ahead of time. Many people simply do not have a workable environment in which they can interview in a quiet space; the library may be able to meet this need.

The Omaha, Nebraska-based community technology opened its Virtual Interview Lab to support a community of local users seeking and interviewing for jobs. They offer tools such as webcam, microphone, and high-speed Internet, and staffers provide support with the setup before a user's interview. In the Toronto Public Library, there are rooms for job seekers and includes a one-hour prep appointment. Toronto City News' Dilshad Burman writes,

> the room comes equipped with a laptop connected to a larger monitor, web cam, headset and ring light. Keeping accessibility in mind, a specialized keyboard with larger font and a track-ball style mouse are also

available. Both the desk and chair are height adjustable to accommodate mobility devices or other physical requirements.[14]

Illinois Institute of Technology Libraries offer interview booths[15] limited to fifteen minutes to two hours using the LibCal booking system, a Springshare product. The room/booth should have electrical outlets and WiFi access, along with good lighting.

Dressing for Success—One of the most important ways to stand out in an interview, at a job fair, or on the first day of work is by dressing up professionally. Libraries can offer free business clothes to users. This requires planning and spacing where there are donated business suits, ties, and shoes from the community.

Known as "career closets" by institutions such as Mount Aloysius College Library & Learning Commons, "the career closet is available for any student who needs professional attire for an interview or starting a new job. The clothing is available at no cost & students are free to keep what they find."[16] It may be worth offering if you have a space where you can store lightly used or brand-new suits. If you like to create donated goods as circulation, the NYPL offers this to adults and teens looking for business clothes and accessories to borrow. Users can search for and borrow neckties, bowties, briefcases, handbags, and more.[17]

Creating Business Cards Workshop—Business cards are essential for sharing contacts and information. Your library may consider hosting a business card workshop so attendees can design their business cards and then select copies that the library can print out if possible. The Denver Public Library shows users how to design their business cards using Microsoft Publisher.[18] If you have makerspace technologies, consider what North Carolina State University Libraries has offered: "Making Your Brand: Create Custom Laser-Cut Business Cards." It is a unique way to get hands-on experience designing custom business cards using laser cutters.[19]

MARKETING YOUR SERVICES AND PROGRAMS

With so many potentially impactful services to be offered by your library, it is important to consider how you market and promote them to your community and users. Here are some marketing suggestions:

E-Newsletters—Consider using e-newsletters such as *Myemma* or *MailChimp*, with which you can create and customize a newsletter focused on career services/programs. In addition, if your library already pushes out newsletters on a monthly or bimonthly basis, consider adding a section dedicated to career and business support. You may also want to highlight quotes from your participants' experiences in such programs. Such testimonies can powerfully inform others about the impact of your services and programs, if participants have found the library's support to be useful.

Flyers—Looking to create printed flyers to share at events or to post in the library? You can create flyers through Canva, Smore, or Piktochart tools that have templates set up. If you do not have a graphic designer/marketing specialist on staff, these tools can help ease the process of creating something simple and efficient.

Social Media Channels—Consider promoting your services on social media channels such as

- Facebook
- X (formerly known as Twitter)
- Instagram
- Threads, an app within Instagram
- Bluesky
- YouTube
- TikTok
- LinkedIn

Short blurbs regarding upcoming sessions will get the word out, and you can track viewer count. For Instagram, you can hold a live Instagram Stories that can be a Q&A conversation with a librarian who might be able to answer questions about career advice or offer suggestions regarding career development utilizing library resources. In addition, for sessions that are held remotely, you can add the recordings to a YouTube channel to be viewed by others later. You will also want to ensure that the closed captioning is on for all your recordings.

YouTube does closed captioning automatically, but it may be worth checking again to confirm. In addition, you can turn these recordings into audio files for sharing in a podcast. Anchor.fm can be the outlet to preserve and disseminate your audio files in a podcast format. It can be an effective marketing tool if you have content to share.

Website—If you want to create a separate space for these activities, consider website designers such as WordPress, Wix, and Weebly. They are easy to design, but the issue is updating these pages to ensure that they remain current. There can also be a dedicated blog space on your library website or a separate page, where your volunteers/career coaches/speakers can share tips, information, or other resources and highlight relevant library programs regarding career development topics.

Newspapers/News Media—Consider putting the information in your community/local newspapers so that others can see it. This information can be added to the newspapers' websites. You will need to consult with the local presses because some may consider the content to be advertisements.

Generally, they are community events. If you have a reporter coming to cover your services, that would be a great major buzz and attention for your library. In Canada, the Edmonton Public Library promoted their "life skill classes" from job interviewing to using in a Global News Morning segment.[20]

Word of Mouth/Business Cards—Traditionally, word of mouth is an effective way to share information. Word of mouth is generally a way that immigrants and businesses owned by immigrants share their experiences with others, as Madeleine Ildefonso from LAPL shared in the Call Number Podcast: "Supporting Small Business," focusing on street vendors.[21] You may enhance this process by creating small business cards about the services that can be shared easily by people passing by in the library. Your library friends group or foundation may also be able to promote your programs and activities. Keep in mind, though, that one bad experience can make users distrust the services/resources. You may want to find a way to gauge people's interest ahead of time.

Incentivizing Participation—The Cleveland Public Library has created a credentialing process as an incentive to go through technology training.[22] This can use a digital badge program to ensure that participants receive a form of validation or recognition of their skills, time, and commitment and provide something they can share on LinkedIn and other web profiles. Some programs that support digital badging might include the following:

- Passport—https://www.openpassport.org/
- Credly—https://info.credly.com/
- Open Badges—https://openbadges.org/
- LinkedIn Learning Certificates—https://www.linkedin.com/learning/

In addition, this type of program can align with future employers or specialized skills to promote transferrable skills and skill building. Margaret Phillips, Heather Howard, and Dave Zwicky of Purdue University Libraries offered a webinar in 2023 called, "Using Digital Badges to Prepare Students for University to Workplace Transition." In this webinar, the speakers described how they developed, assessed, and promoted digital badging modules for undergraduate students on topics related to information literacy and aligning with the workplace skills and expectations such as information gathering strategies, competitive analysis, patent information, industry standards, and informed communication learning.[23] The main takeaway is that with digital badging, it is possible for libraries to incentivize students (and patrons) to learn and develop skills for employment.

You may want to explore the ACT WorkKeys National Career Readiness Certificate (NCRC) page on setting up a digital badge for workforce programs. ACT partners with Credly to issue these badges.[24] The purpose of these digital badges is to easily identify qualified individuals that possess the foundational skills needed across jobs; assess and promote the skills across your communities to attract industry to your region; connect individuals with active job opportunities in your community; securely verify credentials that are portable nationally, statewide, and regionally.

It is important to know your audience that you are marketing your services to. If the groups are specifically immigrant groups, especially non-English-speaking groups, you will need to focus on your marketing resources in those languages.

Libraries Build Business—The Communications Toolkit by the American Library Association (ALA) and Co/lab Capacity is a free and rich resource to help prepare for a communication plan to engage with business support organizations, small business owners, elected officials, policymakers, funders, community decision-makers, and library staff in support of business and entrepreneurship in the community. The templates provided in this toolkit can be a great start in connecting with your identified groups.[25] Some of these resources will be referenced in later chapters.

ASSESSMENT OF PROGRAMMING/SERVICE

We have listed a series of marketing and incentivizing tools. Now to assess the impact of your learning, we will share some ideas in this section. These events related to the workforce and career development are critical in reinforcing the library's efforts and commitment to supporting career services and workforce development.

A key critical component is assessment. You will need to think about how to assess the participation and use the feedback to improve or change your approach to providing such services. Another critical point regarding assessment is that it demonstrates your library's impact on your community and how you may be able to obtain or secure funding for your library. Here are some tools to consider when assessing your services/programs:

General Statistic Collection—There are a lot of numbers you can collect to assess your program; for example:

- How many attendees come to your speakers series events?
- How many users participate in an interview/career coaching session?
- How many books related to career development gets circulated?
- How many databases get used?

These numbers can add up and show you areas to promote or to revisit. You will want to collect statistics for general information to push out in your annual report or newsletters so that others can see the traction of your library's work in this area.

Survey—To understand your services better, consider giving your users a survey with simple questions. This can be integrated into your general assessment program for any event that you normally do. If you want to do something separate, it is possible to keep it very straightforward. These surveys can be deployed toward the end of the session/event. You can do it via paper handouts or online through Google Forms or Survey Monkey. Potential questions can include

- Why did you attend today's event/session?
- How did you hear about today's event/session?
- What did you get out of today's event/session?
- What would you like to know or learn more regarding today's event/session?
- See appendix B for more sample questions.

Focus Group/Interview—In addition to surveys, if your library can hold focus groups/interview sessions with your users, you can find out more about what users get from these sessions. The difference between an interview and a focus group is that an interview is only one-on-one, while a focus group may have two or more people in the session. Sometimes, interviews may be preferred to get to know your library community members individually, and they are easier to manage scheduling-wise. It is best to use focus groups when there are diverse demographics with similar interests to gather feedback. One concern with focus groups is that there may be dominant voices, and you will need to assess and ensure that everyone gets to speak and share their thoughts.

Focus groups can be run in person or remotely. They can be facilitated by a volunteer or by a library staff member. Here are some sample questions:

- For career services/workforce development, what areas should the library consider?
- What types of jobs are you interested in?
- What are some questions you have regarding the job searching process?
- What questions do you have about the library?
- See appendix B for more sample questions.

Library Card to Access Services—One consideration is to ensure that your users can get a library card to access the services/events. The issue is that this can prohibit non-library users from participating in the program, and especially users who know that they have library fines may feel deterred from participating. It is an important consideration to support data collection and tracking, but privacy is also a factor to consider. If the events tend to draw a lot of people, it is best to prioritize those who have library cards, to keep track of and manage the process. It is not ideal but it ensures that you can assess library card users and encourage non-library cardholders to get a library card, too.

Assessment of Technology Usages—Keeping track of using and circulating these technology tools are helpful indicators of importance; in addition, you may want to ask users to share stories of how these tools support their learning, career development, and work. By gathering and sharing these stories, you may be able to promote narratives of positive impact, especially when it comes to funding advocacy work.

CONSULTATIVE SERVICES

One of the most important services to provide is one-on-one services, whereby patrons will feel validated and supported in this setting outside of a classroom. Providing career counseling one-on-one reinforces the patron's trust and relationship with you and the library. In addition to resume/CV/cover letter review and mock interview preps, here are other services that your library may want to consider that will support those who are marginalized and affected negatively in other ways:

Business/Entrepreneurship Support—There are many opportunities to support business/entrepreneurship efforts from small business owners to business students. We cover this in chapter 2.

Applying for Unemployment Benefits Workshops—You may want to host a workshop on how users can apply for unemployment benefits or feature a specialist from your local Department of Employment or Workforce Development or Department of Labor to walk through the process. A staff leading the session may want to learn about the process by investigating ahead of time and be prepared to have materials and contact/referrals for users interested in more information.

In August 2015, the Lake City Library in South Carolina offered an unemployment benefits workshop to help

> unemployed persons learn how to apply for unemployment benefits online. Presented by library staff, the workshop will show participants how to use the South Carolina Department of Employment and Workforce (DEW) website to apply for benefits. This two-hour workshop is free. However, registration is required.[26]

By creating materials and information to be shared with your users, your library proactively supports community members experiencing unemployment.

Expungement Clinic in the Library—People who have been incarcerated will no doubt experience stigma and additional hurdles in adjusting to society, unfortunately. This includes a record of a criminal conviction that can be reviewed as a public record and can hinder those applying for jobs during the background check. The library and its staff are not in a position to provide legal counsel or support. However, the library can consider partnering with organizations such as an advocacy group, law firm, or law school to lessen or possibly remove these barriers for job employment. This process is called "expungement," which is to remove or erase the record.

The American Bar Association defines expungement as

> the process by which a record of criminal conviction is destroyed or sealed from state or federal record. An expungement order directs the court to treat the criminal conviction as if it had never occurred, especially removing it from the defendant's criminal court as well as, ideally the public record.[27]

In a podcast episode hosted by the Public Library Association (PLA), Elena Coelho and Marshall Shord from the Worcester County (MD) Library share their experiences running a bimonthly expungement clinic in an area with a dearth of pro bono resources. They described their partnership with the Maryland Volunteer Lawyers Services and how to enable digital connections for participants to talk with lawyers made available by the library.[28]

In 2023, the St. Louis County Library offered programs and loan technology to formerly incarcerated people to develop business skills—especially because they have a difficult time obtaining business loans from banks. Andrea Y. Henderson from St. Louis Public Radio writes,

> The St. Louis County Library is launching a small-business program to help formerly incarcerated people in the region learn how to become entrepreneurs. The Small Business Launchpad, which starts in August, will provide 12 participants with business planning workshops and expert-led sessions about business financing. The program also will teach people how to develop business ideas, understand pricing and prepare marketing materials.[29]

Read more about this in chapter 2, regarding entrepreneurship.

Legal Support Advice—An employment lawyer may also visit the library to provide advice for community members, to discuss such matters as working within the scope of employment, job description/duties, compensation, and other employment topics. This can be from a partnership with a nonprofit or law firm. In a way, it is a win-win for both groups. You might have free expertise provided by your library, and the organization gains visibility from this promotion. It is important to note that the library and any of its staff should never offer legal advice or guidance.

There was a podcast conversation on this topic from Dr. Steve Albrecht's podcast in the "Library Service, Safety, & Security" section of Library 2.0 Series:

"Course and Scope of Employment: Legal and Fair Work in Your Library." The main takeaways from this podcast:

- Clarify a job description and job duties
- Ensure that job descriptions are up-to-date
- Understand what is legal and not legal; how to understand exempt and nonexempt status

Immigration Consultation Day—The Pew Research Center found that after COVID-19 outbreaks, immigrant naturalizations were on the rise in the United States in 2022.[30] Support for naturalization can be offered in the library via space and connection with nonprofits supporting such immigration services as applying for citizenship and naturalization, employment authorization, green card renewal, adjustment of status, and more. This may not be directly related to career services, but it is certainly connected to workforce development.

Nonprofit organizations such as the Immigration Advocates Network and American Immigration Lawyers Association (AILA) have chapters nationwide that can partner with local libraries to host these services in support of your community members. You will need to market your services multilingually, focusing on your groups' languages, and it is also important to note that many may not visit the library if there are no connections to the communities. You will need to establish that kind of rapport, or your nonprofit partner may already have that presence in the communities. Offering this kind of service can enhance immigrants' connection to the library; focusing on reducing the barriers they experience in seeking employment may be an impactful approach.

Think about resources to communicate with this group of users, whether those may be provided by the library, your city/state government, or nonprofit partners. Madeleine Ildefonso, a senior librarian from the LAPL shared in a "Call Number Podcast: Supporting Small Business," Cell-Ed [cell-ed.com] supports digital and health literacy through the cell phone since she noted that street vendors might use their cell phones to communicate and obtain information.[31] It is important to understand the preferred communication methods to engage with small business owners.

Multilingual Engagement and Support—More than 350 languages are spoken in the United States. Certainly, English is often the concentrated and dominant language. Still, there are other languages to consider when reaching out to groups who may not be familiar with your services and to foster engagement with such groups. It is critical to hire bilingual staff who reflect the communities' needs. Librarian Nicholas Brown (2022) makes these important points in his web article, "Three Lessons for Launching Successful Multilingual Programs at Your Library":[32]

- Hire bilingual administrative staff on programming, outreach, and communications teams who have a wider view of everything the system is doing, across all the branches.
- Make bilingual skills part of the job search and requirements.
- Provide a pay incentive for staff who help translate library materials outside of their regular duties.

Overall, table 1.1 lists the services you may want to consider hosting in your library and a brief description of the types of services:

Overall, partnerships are critical to support the community of users and their interests. Many libraries have also partnered with vendors to provide these services; these can be effective ways to support your community consistently.

COLLECTION DEVELOPMENT AND DATABASES

Collection development is key in supporting workforce development. There are many free and subscription resources that your library can consider. Most importantly, forming collections-building partnerships may help support career development and learning. You may want to partner with your state library (in the United States), if there are offerings whereby your community members can benefit via public libraries. These resources can also be shared with academic libraries, to encourage users to get their public library cards.

Partnerships are critical to increase resources and support. For example, the California State Library created partnerships with vendors to offer tools that can support learning for community users called CAreer Pathways through public libraries.[33]

> The California State Library supports various workforce development platforms for all Californians through their local public libraries. Public libraries are community hubs that bring people together and close the opportunity gap by connecting people to essential services and resources. The resources available through CAreer Pathways are another way in which libraries aid in personal economic development, increase digital equity, and support the information needs of a 21st Century society.[34]

These tools include Coursera, GetSetUp, Job & Career Accelerator, Learning Express Library, LinkedIn Learning, Northstar, Skillshare, and VetNOW.

For other databases, we will explore general ones that are potentially useful or supportive for your teaching/learning purposes. For specific ones, especially business-related ones, consider chapter 2, and for an extensive list of others. Table 1.1 provides a sample list of library workshops and their descriptions that you may want to offer.

Table 1.1 List of Library Workshops and Their Descriptions

Sample Library Workshops	Sample Workshop Descriptions
LinkedIn workshop	LinkedIn is a popular social media site where you can connect with others across industries, learn more about job opportunities, and get recruited. (If your library has LinkedIn Learning you may want to share how this library provided resource works.)
Building a professional webpage	Learn how to create a professional website that showcases your portfolio, resume, work experiences and accomplishments, and more.
Computer basics and using the Internet	Interested in developing basic computer skills? This workshop covers how to learn computer basics and navigate the website effectively.
Microsoft Office	This workshop highlights how to use MS Office tools such as Microsoft Word, Excel, and PowerPoint.
Google Drive Suite	This workshop highlights how to use Google Drive Suite effectively such as Google Docs, Google Sheets, and Slide.
Project management tools	There are many free versions of project management tools. If you are currently working on a project and need help managing the project, consider attending the workshop to learn about different tools to consider.
Job searching	Learn different tools and search engines specifically for jobs meeting your interest. We will explore search strategies in managing the job searching process. Prerequisite: Basic computer and Internet skills.
Cover letter support	Learn how to create a resume through a template that you can take back for any job opportunities you are seeking. Prerequisite: Basic computer skills.
Resume building support	Learn how to create a resume through a template that you can take back for any job opportunities you seek. Prerequisite: Basic computer skills.
Networking 101	Not a fan of networking? Not sure what it is? Come learn the secrets of networking and how to be a connector. You will learn how to use these skills during your job search process and to expand your network.
Library resources supporting you for a new job today	In this workshop, we review several library resources that can support your learning. Whether you are interested in getting a certificate in cybersecurity or brushing up your communication skills, there are plenty of online learning resources that we will go over (these tools can be Coursera, Udemy, and LinkedIn Learning).
Using social media to create a brand	Learn how to use social media tools such as Facebook, X (formerly Twitter), Instagram, YouTube, and TikTok to help promote your business and brand.

(Continued)

Table 1.1 (Continued)

Sample Library Workshops	Sample Workshop Descriptions
Find, get, and succeed your internship	Learn how to find internships for your specific majors and identify resources to prepare for your internships.
Money management skills	Starting a new job? Learn how to manage financial skills and budgeting.
Dress to impress on a budget	Need tips to dress properly for your upcoming interview or job?
Writing personal statements: Ideas and resources	Planning to go to graduate school? Learn how to craft a successful personal statement for your application.
Learn salary negotiation skills	Need to negotiate for a desirable salary? Learn tips and tricks to negotiate when you are able to get a new job.
Information interviews	Learn how to be successful in informational interviewing conversations with professionals from other industries and how to accelerate your job search to make it more efficient and to grow your professional network.

In addition to career development and skill training, education support can be a critical part of one's learning. For example, the California State Library offers "The Career Online High School Program" in partnership with California public libraries.

> The Career Online High School Program enables California adults to earn a high school diploma, free of charge, through their local public library. [Since 2022], 27,357 have explored interest in the Career Online High School program, while 6,069 individuals have enrolled in the program. Over 15 percent of Californians over age 25 did not complete their secondary education. Many Career Online High School participants faced barriers in obtaining a high school diploma, including transportation limitations, family responsibilities, restrictive schedules, and educational trauma.[35]

From 2021 to 2022, over seventy public libraries in California offered support for adults to earn a high school diploma through online study via Career Online High School. This resource can also include specific vocational training.

At the SDPL, participants can also enroll in courses in office management, retail customer service, manufacturing, security professional, hospitality and leisure, home career professional, food and hospitality, commercial driving, child care, or general career path preparation in addition to obtaining their high school diploma.[36]

Career Services and Job Centers in Libraries   **19**

Kristina Garcia, Librarian, Adult High School Diploma Program, City of San Diego, SDPL, shared,

> The Adult High School diploma program has been a great addition to the non-traditional services of our organization and illustrates perfectly the San Diego Public Library's mission of inspiring lifelong learning through connections to knowledge and each other. The flexibility of an online program available to students 24/7 to complete their studies around other life responsibilities is a key factor for its success. We are proud of the many graduates who have been able to move forward with their educational and professional goals by taking the initiative to "go back" to high school and complete their coursework.

These partnerships and support might be helpful with marketing and assessment. In addition, they all rely on technology skills, access, and a stable Internet connection. Here are some items to consider regarding technology loans in your library when supporting career development:

Laptop Computer—Loaning laptops can be a complex process. They are generally popular in universities and select public libraries. They are great for supporting those who do not have access to such technologies and need them for work-related purposes. The downside of managing this device is that you will need to regularly update software to ensure that they are ready for use. Computers can also become outdated within a few years due to rapid usage or increasing new technologies.

Web Camera—Most computers have web cameras built-in, but sometimes they may be faulty for whatever reason. A web camera could provide your user to prepare for a work meeting or upcoming interview.

Ring Light—Popular during the pandemic, a ring light is a lighting tool that is commonly used for digital photography and live video sessions; it provides good lighting and can show the person's face more clearly. It also comes in different sizes. This is especially useful for those with an interview coming up via a virtual setting on Zoom or Google Teams.

Microphone—Sound quality is very important. You may offer a tool such as the snowball mic, which can record and project the range of frequencies. In general, all laptops have built-in microphones but sometimes an external one might be useful as a backup. You may also consider headphones with built-in microphones, especially for those who do not have a designated quiet space to speak virtually.

WiFi Hotspot—Another popular item during the pandemic, especially in colleges and universities where hotspot devices were loaned out to students and community members to make it possible to access the Internet remotely. The downside of this device is the monthly subscription cost and usage. It is not quite affordable, but if you can provide hotspots, they will especially support those who are impacted by lack of broadband access and digital exclusion. Of course, technology loans and policies should also consider privacy needs and ensure that user data is discarded after the user has returned the equipment.

Calendar Management Software—How do you manage people's appointments? One consideration is using web tools such as Calendly to manage the booking process. Some institutions use Springshare's LibCal; others may have a built-in system through a calendar. These tools are essential to help keep track of your users.

NEEDS ASSESSMENT

If you are thinking of creating a position to support career development and workforce training, what kind of support do you need for this position to thrive? You will need to check for learning opportunities (more on chapter 4 for classes/courses) and identify community support. Table 1.2 lists sample Needs Assessment using a SWOT analysis that you can consider using along with questions to consider.

SWOT analysis enables you to strategically align this position or expected duties, connecting to and identifying internal and external values and issues. It is best to do this in a group to discuss its relevance and needs since starting a position and recruiting can be a long process.

Strengths include what assets or existing factors enable this position's strength. Weakness is what are the existing factors that point to the position's

Table 1.2 A SWOT Analysis Chart. Question: Should We Create a Position Focusing on Career Services and Workforce Development?

Strengths	Weaknesses
• The position can communicate its engagement using current existing services from the library. • There are in-demand services for job seekers, and this position can immediately support user needs.	• Building relationships takes time, and it may be difficult • The budget is always changing; will this position be sustainable?

Opportunities	Threats
• This position will engage with job seekers and support workforce development programs. • The impact of this role can be useful to demonstrate to funders and stakeholders the library's commitment to workforce development	• Will we find a candidate who can fulfill the community's expectations? • Job needs keep evolving, and demands are changing; how will this individual/position keep up?

weakness. Threats are external issues that may challenge this position, and opportunities are external opportunities that this position may pursue. The SWOT analysis chart is one methodological tool to brainstorm as a team for any position.

ALTERNATIVE TO POSITIONS

It is important to note that some libraries may refer this type of work to vendors or online resources to support career services for various reasons such as lack of resources or capacity and avoiding duplicating efforts. For example, public libraries may partner with organizations such as NOVAworks, a nonprofit, federally funded employment and training agency, to provide career support services for their communities. Representatives from this organization would have drop-in sessions for community members to learn more about such programs and meet with a career advisor or seek training. In chapter 2, we talk a bit more about partnerships. Other libraries like Redwood City Library listed resources as well:

- Online Learning: brush up on job skills and improve your experience level for resumes
- JobNow: Job coaching, resume lab, unemployment assistance, and interview resources and tips
- GFCLearnfree.org: Careers, technology, mobile apps, and learning videos
- Looking for a job? Top Ten Local List from Redwood City Library [PDF]
- Advice for teens that are seeking jobs: Jobs for Teens HQ[37]

There are pros and cons to each approach and you and your team will need to decide how to best support your workforce development program and community of job seekers and employers.

JOB ADVERTISEMENTS AND EXAMPLES TEMPLATE

After you have done a SWOT analysis with your teams, it is important to note that creating a dedicated position for workforce development or career services may require focusing on specific duties within current ones. This section covers public and academic libraries focusing on this position. For public libraries, it is to connect to adult services librarians and a position that focuses on entrepreneurship and engagement with community businesses.

Here are examples from job descriptions that came out recently that summarize key job duties and terminology that you can consider adapting. For academic libraries, business librarians play a natural role in collaborating with career centers and supporting the work of career centers as liaisons. Some other positions might be connected to student services/student success roles, and their work may also align with career centers.

We provide templates here for you to review, adapt, and consider why a dedicated position might be helpful in engaging with your workforce community with this specific need.

Generative AI tools such as ChatGPT might be useful in brainstorming the skills and details of the position. We found the output regarding career services librarian to be interesting from ChatGPT.

A Career Services or Workforce Development Librarian plays a crucial role in assisting library patrons, typically within an academic or public library setting, to effectively navigate their career paths and develop essential skills for employment. Their primary responsibilities encompass a wide range of tasks aimed at supporting individuals in their professional growth and job-seeking endeavors. Here are some key responsibilities of a Career Services or Workforce Development Librarian:

- Career Counseling: Librarians in this role provide one-on-one or group career counseling sessions to help individuals assess their skills, interests, and goals. They assist patrons in exploring various career options, identifying potential industries, and formulating actionable career plans.
- Resume and Cover Letter Assistance: Librarians assist patrons in creating compelling and tailored resumes and cover letters that highlight their qualifications and experiences. They provide guidance on formatting, content, and key skills that employers seek.
- Job Search Strategies: Librarians help patrons develop effective job search strategies, including utilizing online job boards, networking platforms, and company websites. They educate individuals on advanced search techniques and provide resources for identifying job opportunities.
- Interview Preparation: Librarians offer guidance on interview techniques, conduct mock interviews, and provide feedback to help patrons improve their interview skills. They may also share insights on common interview questions, appropriate attire, and follow-up etiquette.
- Skill Development: Librarians assist patrons in acquiring or enhancing job-related skills, such as digital literacy, computer software proficiency, communication skills, and problem-solving abilities. They may curate and recommend online resources, tutorials, and workshops to support skill development.
- Professional Development Workshops: Librarians organize and facilitate workshops, seminars, and training sessions on topics such as resume writing, interview skills, job search strategies, networking, and personal branding.
- Networking Support: Librarians encourage patrons to build professional networks and provide guidance on effective networking strategies, both

online and in person. They may suggest attending industry events, joining professional organizations, and utilizing social media platforms for networking.
- Resource Management: Librarians curate and maintain a collection of up-to-date resources related to career development, job searching, industry trends, and professional growth. They ensure that patrons have access to relevant books, articles, databases, and online tools.
- Collaboration: Librarians collaborate with other library staff, academic departments, local businesses, community organizations, and career centers to enhance the availability of resources and opportunities for patrons.
- Assessment and Evaluation: Librarians assess the effectiveness of their career services initiatives through data collection, surveys, and feedback from patrons. They use this information to improve and tailor their services to better meet the needs of the community.
- Stay Updated: Librarians stay current with industry trends, labor market changes, and emerging technologies to provide accurate and relevant information to patrons.

Overall, the role of a Career Services or Workforce Development Librarian is to empower individuals by equipping them with the knowledge, skills, and resources needed to successfully navigate the ever-evolving job market and achieve their career aspirations.

Job descriptions based on formerly advertised positions (institutions' names and locations are redacted):

Job Example #1 for Public Libraries

For a standard position, this job advertisement provides the language:

Title: Reference Librarian/Adult Services Librarian/Community Engagement Librarian/Workforce Development Librarian/Career Services Librarian

Position Overview: Delivers library programs and services with an emphasis on specialized reference work and professional knowledge and experience in the area of career and workforce development.

Salary: [should be listed and aligned with the range that is expected for your area]

Responsibilities:

- Engage with the public on a variety of topics, including library resources, computer and technology training skills and usage, and other skill-building programs focused on patrons seeking career or business-related information; collaborate with employers to develop programming for job-seeking community interest.

- Participate in developing and delivering outreach, program, and instruction activities focusing on career and workforce development in the library or in the community.
- Organize and be responsible for oral presentations and written reports assigned within the department as needed.
- Build and cultivate relationships with relevant groups, organizations, and institutions, and offer career counseling, coaching, job search assistance, or interview preparations.
- Perform advanced reference services using specialized knowledge to support career and workforce development—may include business information, government information, workforce sectors, skill-building, online learning, and technology resources in person or online.
- Select materials (digital and print) in support of career and workforce development as part of the library's collection; ongoing evaluation and maintenance in the usage and promote access to these materials as needed.

Qualifications:

- A master's degree in library and information science from an ALA-accredited library school; bachelor's degree from a recognized college or university
- Relevant subject knowledge
- Two or more years of appropriate library professional experience or any equivalent combination of education, experience, and training
- Proficiency in a second language other than English is desirable

Job Example #2 for Public Libraries

An alternative to a dedicated librarian position is to hire a career coach that takes on a similar role but entirely focused in the workforce program. Here is an example:

Title: Career Coach

Position Overview: This position supports all aspects of job search, career coaching, and the development of library users. The library serves all job seekers and specializes in helping reentry, career changers, veterans, and fifty-five plus adults.

Responsibilities:

- Support and assist with the job search process, including email and LinkedIn setup; support Internet navigation, including job search process; and uploading/downloading documents into employment systems.

- Support and assist in writing resumes, cover letters, and CVs.
- Prepare patrons with job interview tactics, host mock interviews, and offer guidance.
- Identify and recruit professionals to participate in career or industry-specific interview panels and programming.
- Provide classroom instruction and one-on-one consultation on career-specific library databases.
- Create and offer workshops and career events such as workshop materials, flyers, and other documents.
- Support community outreach to promote and increase public awareness and participation and use of library services.

Qualifications:

- Bachelor's degree with a minimum two years of relevant work experience.
- Demonstrated public services experience delivering career services with the ability to work with diverse patrons.
- Strong computer skills and knowledge using Microsoft Office and Google products.
- Experience in mentoring, coaching, or advising role.
- Comfortable providing advice, feedback, and critiques professionally for individuals and in groups.
- Ability to create plans to support personal and career growth.
- Ability to speak another language strongly designed.
- Excellent problem-solving, decision-making, and time management skills.
- Familiar with employment and job training services in the community.

Job Example #3 for Academic Libraries

Business librarian position may directly connect to career or workforce development but the goal is to align these areas closely. Although they are not specified, you may need to include that in your description. Here is an example:

Title: Business/Hospitality College Librarian

Position Overview: The university seeks a librarian with an ALA-accredited master's degree in library or information science or international equivalent. The position will liaise with the career services center, college of business, hospitality, and other academic departments or programs. The librarian will participate in reference, research, and teaching services in the library. The librarian also advises students, faculty, and staff on research projects through in-person or online consultations; the librarian will be responsible for creating and maintaining research and course guides; and the librarian will participate in library and institutional committees and professional associations.

Responsibilities:

- Actively serve as the main liaison to the college of business and hospitality and career services center.
- Teach library and research instruction in the college of business and provide consultation to faculty, staff, and students about research projects in departments as assigned.
- Present information sessions and library orientations to departmental faculty and other groups.
- Create and maintain subject guides and course guides in various media.
- Provide subject-specific reference and research services in person and virtually.
- Serve on library, university, and professional committees.

Qualifications:

- ALA-accredited master's degree in library or information science or international equivalent.
- Excellent oral and written communication skills.
- Demonstrated experience and commitment to teaching and library instruction and public service.
- Ability to work cooperatively and collaboratively with coworkers and campus community.
- Graduate or undergraduate business degree desired.
- Professional experience working with postsecondary business students.

Job Example #4: ChatGPT 3.5 Created Position

ChatGPT, a generative AI tool from OpenAI, was used to create a position and here is what it came up with:

Title: Career Services Librarian

Are you passionate about helping individuals achieve their professional aspirations? Do you have a deep appreciation for the role of education and information in career development? If so, we have an exciting opportunity for you!

Position: Career Services Librarian Location: [City, State] Application Deadline: [Date]

About Us: We are a vibrant and forward-thinking [City/University/Institution] dedicated to fostering lifelong learning and empowering our community to excel in their careers. We believe that access to quality career services and resources is crucial for personal and professional growth.

Position Overview: As a Career Services Librarian, you will play a pivotal role in supporting individuals as they navigate their career journeys. You will collaborate with students, alumni, and community members to provide comprehensive career guidance, connect them with relevant resources, and empower them to make informed decisions about their futures. This role offers a unique opportunity to blend your passion for librarianship with your enthusiasm for career development.

Responsibilities:

- Develop, organize, and deliver career-focused workshops, seminars, and events.
- Provide one-on-one career counseling and advising sessions to individuals at various stages of their careers.
- Curate and maintain an up-to-date collection of career-related materials, including books, databases, and online resources.
- Collaborate with faculty and staff to integrate career development resources into academic programs.
- Stay current with industry trends, labor market information, and emerging technologies to enhance career services.
- Foster partnerships with employers, alumni networks, and industry associations to facilitate networking and job placement opportunities.
- Assist individuals with resume and cover letter writing, interview preparation, job searching, and professional branding.
- Collect and analyze data to assess the effectiveness of career services and make data-driven improvements.

Qualifications:

- Master's degree in library and information science from an accredited institution.
- Strong understanding of career development theories and practices.
- Excellent interpersonal and communication skills.
- Experience in providing career services, counseling, or advising is preferred.
- Familiarity with online job search platforms, career assessment tools, and resources.
- Ability to work collaboratively in a dynamic and diverse environment.
- Innovative mindset and willingness to embrace technology for enhancing services.

Benefits:

- Competitive salary and benefits package.
- Professional development opportunities.

- Access to extensive library resources and research databases.
- Engaging and inclusive work environment.

Application Process: Interested candidates are invited to submit their resume, cover letter, and references by [Application Deadline] to [Application Email/Link]. Please include "Career Services Librarian Application" in the subject line.

Join us in shaping the future of career services and making a lasting impact on the lives of individuals in our community. Apply today and embark on a rewarding journey of mentorship, growth, and empowerment.

[City/University/Institution] is an equal opportunity employer. All qualified applicants will receive consideration for employment without regard to race, color, religion, sex, sexual orientation, gender identity, national origin, disability, or veteran status.

INTERVIEWS AND PROFILES

In this section of the chapter, we interview librarians who have implemented career services in their institutions. These profiles are meant to give you an idea of what work entails for this support and collaboration.

An Interview with Marzena Ermler, Assistant Director (Brooklyn Office), New York University and formerly Career Services Manager at the NYPL

Question 1: How did you support career-seeking community members in your library?

Marzena: Throughout my coaching practice, I aim to meet each job seeker wherever they are in their job search journey, paying attention to their backgrounds and life circumstances. The same philosophy I also introduced to the NYPL's Career Services team consisting of four outstanding staff members and truly amazing volunteer career coaches, who, as industry experts and recruiters, were significantly stretching the capacity of our team. During the pandemic, in addition to career coaching, I introduced resilience coaching to help our patrons deal with other life issues that were piling up on top of a need for a job.

The coaching support was also anchored in the robust offering of workshops provided in person and virtually, where invited industry experts shared their insights on various aspects of job search techniques, such as creating the most impactful marketing materials (resumes, cover letters, LinkedIn profiles), finding the hidden job market through networking or crafting impactful responses to the usual and less common interview questions. As an observer or facilitator of these sessions, I saw how helpful it was for the job seekers to know that they were not alone in the job search process and that other people had similar questions and issues to handle. These workshops also made the participants realize what to concentrate on during their career coaching appointments to accelerate their individual job search process. During coaching appointments, I would also direct job seekers to various databases, Vault and Career Cruising being the most popular for career guides and self-assessments to create more self-awareness regarding work preferences and industry information.

Question 2: What is a tool that you commonly refer to or use?
Marzena: As I mentioned before, Vault and Career Cruising are my two favorite databases. Patrons can access them with a library card, but completely open to all is the Occupational Outlook Catalog created by the U.S. Bureau of Labor Statistics with information on jobs, educational opportunities, and other job search tools. To understand how an Applicant Tracking System handles a resume during an online application process, I recommend jobscan.co. A word of caution here is that initially, the website will allow one or two resume scans for free. Still, if you want to keep using it as a diagnostic tool to measure your resume's alignment with a particular job description, you must pay a membership fee.

Question 3: What is often the most common issue that community members experience?
Marzena: No matter your life or professional experience, looking for a job or an internship can be very stressful. Job seekers of all ages often feel intimidated by the myriad of job search tasks they need to accomplish, and they need clarification on sometimes conflicting advice they receive. Connecting with others during events at your library or your college provides the opportunity to be reassured that you are not facing a job search alone and that there are services and tools to help you succeed. And the cliché expression that looking for a job is a job in itself is definitely true, which could be disheartening, but I often encourage my coaches to reframe this thought and consider the job search as an opportunity to concentrate and reflect on themselves; their values, goals, motivations, which we, in general, don't do when we have a full-time job.

Question 4: Do you engage with employers or companies? If so, how?
Marzena: During my time at the library, I have created partnerships with local employers to connect job seekers with opportunities during large-scale in-person and virtual job fairs, where patrons could speak directly to hiring managers or H.R. representatives without going through lengthy online application forms. I also organized small-scale hiring events, usually hosting one or two employers that needed to hire many new staff, for example, for seasonal service or retail jobs.

An invaluable for job seekers was a collaboration I started with the Workforce One Centers offering access to employers and other services connected to the Labor Department. Because of our overlapping goals and constituencies, an essential aspect of this collaboration was the mutual cross-advertising of programs offered by the Library, the Centers, and the Labor Department.

Currently, at NYU very popular on the employers' side, and the students' side are visits to the local employers. This is an excellent opportunity for students to have a closer look at the company's inner workings, including the company's culture and physical offices. Employers are also interested in attracting a bright and well-educated workforce to their companies and potentially shortening the costly interviewing process.

Question 5: What advice do you have for libraries supporting job seekers?
Marzena: Job search support is a service needed by library patrons no matter what the economy is doing to the job market at a given time. It provides a very concrete ability for a library to positively influence patrons' lives at various stages of their career, starting with teaching high schoolers how to create good resumes often without having any significant work experience to helping seasoned professionals transition from one job to another or to reenter the workforce after a break. In a good economy, it is hard to advocate for securing dedicated resources (primarily staff) to develop library career services, and it is easier to refer patrons to other non for profit organizations providing similar services. This is a rather short-sighted approach because, as we know, the economy is cyclical, and when it is weak, and people start losing jobs, it is also more challenging to find funds in library budgets to build career services.

I also see library career services as a "high touch" service where library staff interact with patrons on a deeply personal level, often discussing very private matters that are usually not handled during typical interactions in a library setting. Therefore library leadership should provide library staff working in career services with appropriate staff development opportunities to equip them with career coaching tools and skills.

It is also essential for libraries to create partnerships with other organizations that provide career services to develop a network of offerings for job seekers who often have particular challenges (immigration status, disability, reentry, underserved, etc.) stemming from their salient identities and backgrounds.

An Interview with Lateka Grays, Hospitality & Career Services Librarian, Associate Professor at the University of Las Vegas, Nevada (UNLV)

Question 1: Can you tell us a bit about your role? How do you support career-seeking community members in your library at UNLV ?
Lateka: I am the liaison between the UNLV Libraries and the career services professionals on the campus of the University of Nevada, Las Vegas. I am a Certified Career Services Provider (CCSP) through the National Career Development Association (NCDA) and a Gallup Certified Strengths Coach. I am responsible for curating collections that support career development for

students and for staff. I teach workshops related to the resources and create outreach experiences. I am a member of our newly formed career champions group, the Rebel Career Champions Network (RCCN). "They are liaisons for their college, school, or unit who help to educate and share information about the RCCN with colleagues and students, and who share their college/school/unit's workforce, curricular, and career preparation events, activities, and resources with the Network."

Question 2: What is a tool that you commonly refer to or use?
Lateka: Given my coaching status, I administer the CliftonStrengths assessment frequently. It is a tool to help individuals identify themes related to their talents. In the career resources, I include materials that align with the career competencies established by a task force for the UNLV Provost's Office. I was a member of the group and contributed to the work to establish the competencies. This also includes graduate and professional school preparation, on-the-job success resources, affinity group career resources, and life design materials. These materials are in-print and online.

Question 3: How do you engage with your learners on career research services? What is often the most common issue that students experience when it comes to career research?
Lateka: As previously mentioned, I conduct workshops related to career literacy like researching potential employers and opportunities in their chosen career field. I have also assisted with resume and LinkedIn profile reviews and mock interviews. The undergraduate students that I meet are often uncertain about the formatting of their career documents like the cover letter, resume, and LinkedIn profile. They often receive conflicting or generalized information and need to conduct research about preferred formats for their industry. They struggle with introductions or "elevator pitches" and tend to wait too late to begin thinking about career-related options. Students also overlook many of the great experiences that they have engaged in and miss translating those experiences on their resumes. My role is to refer them to the appropriate career professionals on campus and provide resources with additional credible examples.

Question 4: Do you partner with UNLV Career Services? If so, can you tell us about your partnership with them?
Lateka: In addition to my collection development work, I teach workshops and host career-related events to support UNLV students and alumni. I also helped establish our communication group to share information because we have a decentralized career infrastructure with a main office and departmental offices. The ability to share information facilitates collaboration across departments to better leverage resources and expertise. I also offer coaching related

to the CliftonStrengths assessment. I have recently become a facilitator with our campus human resources learning series due to networking with career and workforce development colleagues.

Question 5: What advice do you have for academic libraries supporting students who are job seekers?
Lateka: Identify your gaps whether that be your own skillset or the collections within the libraries. I pursued the certifications previously mentioned to gain a foundation in the theories and work within the career and workforce development industry. Reach out to career colleagues to better understand their needs. If funding is available, I attend career-related conferences or other professional development to remain current with trends in the career-development space. I also go on business tours, if invited to understand the needs of employers who hire our graduates. I have found them to be welcoming and also surprised about the resources and expertise that we offer. This has helped to get a seat at the table to become a collaborative partner.

An Interview with Elizabeth Joseph, Assistant Director, New Rochelle Public Library, New York

Question 1: Can you tell us about your work and role in the library field? How do you support career-seeking community members in the libraries where you work and have worked?
Elizabeth: I have spent my two-decade long career as a librarian in urban, public libraries. I found that this environment has allowed me to use my passion and skills to guide people on their journey to self-actualization.

The first step to helping job seekers is the reference interview. This interaction is critical to understanding the career and learning needs of the patron before providing access to resources. Generally, following that initial contact, we refer the patron to the Book-a-Librarian service. During this appointment, the librarian provides a survey of appropriate print and digital resources and suggests next steps. Follow-up appointments will be a review of careering opportunities across various platforms. Subsequent appointments can be made to review resumes, cover letters and application documents.

We offer requisite technology for personal use that is outfitted with resume and cover letter templates. We provide coaching sessions with volunteer career counselors. The volunteer counselors come from calls for community experts and partnerships with several nonprofit and public agencies. These include Department of Labor, Goodwill Career Centers and Community opportunity programs. This invaluable service to patrons provides not only critiques of resumes and cover letters but also mock interviews. We also have a select team of community volunteers who provide advice on a career path best suited for particular interest, skill and personality.

Resources and career coaching aside, the library also hosts career fairs featuring local and seasonal employers. Job seekers can use this opportunity to meet and network with potential hiring firms.

As lifelong learning institutions, libraries must always be aware of continuing professional learning needs and so we also offer a wide array of professional development workshops, lectures and seminars so that our users are optimized for future promotional opportunities.

Question 2: What has your experience been like in setting up a program plan and training, and getting buy-in internally in libraries to create career services or workforce development programs for your communities? Any advice for readers who might want to start one in their libraries?

Elizabeth: External forces such as the economic crisis of the 2000s and the COVID pandemic forced the creation and renewal of the library's career programming and services.

Once the need is established, we begin with a persuasive presentation to the library administration. The presentation details program design which integrates elements of costs, staffing, partnerships and the outline of services we will provide. Another major component of the justification is feedback framework that will be utilized as well as the outcomes we aspire to achieve. We use a similar slide deck and pitch when seeking partnerships and funding.

Workforce development programs must not be created in siloes. It's important to share the program details with the entire staff so that it will be promoted accordingly.

The success of the career services program is contingent on proper advertising and marketing of the program to pertinent clientele, groups, community organizations and on media platforms. While numerical data is essential to understanding program performance, it's equally important to use the data to tell a larger story about the objectives accomplished. Additionally, the amplification and publication of success stories is an integral part of its longevity.

Agility is key to the success of workforce development programs because if program features and aspects don't yield the intended results, then you must pause and reflect on what is working and what is not. This exercise is important to developing a program that effectively addresses the needs of patrons.

Question 3: Can you tell us the importance of advocacy work in securing funding for these library projects related to workforce development? What are your strategies for speaking with stakeholders about the importance of libraries supporting small business owners, entrepreneurs, and the economy?

Elizabeth: Public Libraries play a major role in safeguarding a community's vitality and economic success. A strong and thriving workforce is critical to a town's growth.

Our pitch and press kits highlight the savings our program provides individuals and communities. We also echo its value and positive impact at every stakeholder meeting and gathering. We create both physical and digital program assets to display and distribute at all various community gatherings and facilities.

We format our statistical data into visuals that stakeholders, funders and government officials can understand and appreciate. We tell stories and share testimonies from library users who have benefited from our programs. We utilize a variety of communications platforms to broadcast the success including social media posts, press releases and postings in various community newsletters.

It's vital that library staff are always ambassadors of the program and be prepared to share the details of the program including statistics and goals achieved.

Question 4: What about specific small business owners such as Black, Indigenous, People of Color (BIPOC) and women, what are your thoughts, and activities, and strategies on how libraries can support them and their businesses based on your experiences or what you have seen?

Elizabeth: Library staff must be well trained and possess not just cultural competence but also cultural humility. We are intentional about our outreach and program design so that our programs and services are relevant to the needs of women, Black, Latino, BIPOC and people with disabilities. We know that each of these groups are not a monolith and treat each person as an individual with unique needs. We actively seek out speakers and organizational partner representatives so that they mirror the identities and lived experiences of our diverse population. We pursue and strive for programs that possess personal relevance and significance.

Question 5: Anything else we did not get to talk about that you want to share?

Elizabeth: Libraries must understand and adapt to the gig economy landscape and adjust programs and services as per those trends. We must be aware and current about technology and its implications to the workforce. We must be knowledgeable about how AI, Robotics, autonomous vehicles and other emerging technologies can disrupt employment across various sectors and industries. It's important to not just assemble and hold on to this knowledge but to share it with colleagues, stakeholders, community leaders. A living wage that supports the individual and their family is a basic human right and libraries as public institutions must contribute to that endeavor and commit to building a fair and equitable society.

CHAPTER SUMMARY

This chapter highlighted many areas to consider, including the tools, services, and resources available for such a position focused on workforce development and career services. From marketing to assessment to specific services to interview profiles and job advertisements, this chapter offered a general overview of different resources. Takeaways include

- Market your services to your communities
- Focus on technology resources and databases
- Partner with communities interested in workforce development
- Analyze and brainstorm the need for this position
- Create dedicated positions to support this work
- Interview and Profiles of Librarians Supporting Workforce Development Programs.

NOTES

1. Wiley. "The State of the Student: Adjusting to the 'New Normal'. . . and All That Comes with It." February 13, 2023. Accessed at https://www.wiley.com/en-us/network/trending-stories/the-state-of-the-student-adjusting-to-the-new-normal-and-all-that-comes-with-it.
2. Wigert, Ben. "The Future of Hybrid Work: 5 Key Questions Answered with Data." March 15, 2023. Accessed at https://www.gallup.com/workplace/390632/future-hybrid-work-key-questions-answered-data.aspx.
3. Vanek Smith, Stacey. "Workers are Changing Jobs and Getting Raises, and Still Struggling Financially." *NPR*, September 22, 2022. Accessed at https://www.npr.org/2022/09/22/1124118203/workers-are-changing-jobs-and-getting-raises-and-still-struggling-financially.
4. ACT. "Nearly Half of High School Seniors in the 'COVID Cohort' Say Pandemic Affected College Or Career Choices." June 7, 2023. Accessed at https://leader-shipblog.act.org/2023/06/covid-college-choices.html.
5. Bobek, Becky L., and Joyce Z. Schnieders. "Influence of the Coronavirus Pandemic on High School Seniors' Views: College and Career Choices, Challenges, and Opportunities." June 2023. Accessed at https://www.act.org/content/dam/act/secured/documents/Covid-Influence-on-College-and-Career-Choices.pdf.
6. Mount Aloysius College. "LibGuide: Career Development: Career Fair Preparation." June 28, 2023. Accessed at https://libguides.mtaloy.edu/c.php?g=691402&p=6593635.
    Meier, Kelly S. "How to Organize a Successful Job Fair." *Chron*, August 8, 2018. Accessed at https://work.chron.com/organize-successful-job-fair-7647.html.
7. Mount Aloysius College. "LibGuide: Career Development: Career Fair Preparation." June 28, 2023. Accessed at https://libguides.mtaloy.edu/c.php?g=691402&p=6593635.
8. Springfield-Greene County Library District. "Book a Speaker." September 17, 2023. Accessed at https://thelibrary.org/services/speaker.cfm.

9. ACRL Instruction Section Virtual Engagement. "Best Practices for Hosting Virtual Events." April 2023. Accessed at https://docs.google.com/document/d/1pgBC-hWe1v_lqUxofzNVBhEjvNL-TJ4E6yBOmj62yjU/preview#heading=h.k8n32bs2pfqo.
10. Redwood City Public Library. "Human Library." Accessed at https://www.redwoodcity.org/departments/library/events/human-library-2.
11. City of Camarillo Public Library. "RFBC Digital Headshots." December 1, 2022. Accessed at https://camarillolibrary.libcal.com/event/9876669.
12. Freeman, Emmanuel. "TSU Makes Taking Student Portrait Easy With First Self-Serve Innovative Professional Photo Booth." *The Tennessee Tribune*, October 14, 2021. Accessed at https://tntribune.com/tsu-makes-taking-student-portrait-easy-with-first-self-serve-innovative-professional-photo-booth/.
13. Stewart, Emily. "Job Interviews Are a Nightmare—and Only Getting Worse." *Vox*, January 12, 2023. Accessed at https://www.vox.com/the-goods/2023/1/12/23546379/job-interviewing-applying-exhausting-tests-employment?fbclid=IwAR1iHyBO-IX8Je2xOBU3xZYU0pwjDlCL27rdRINUVHrGszcH7Fqxa_8h6aQ&mibextid=Zxz2cZ.
14. Burman, Dilshad. "Toronto Public Library Piloting Virtual Interview Rooms for Job Seekers." *CityNews*, September 15, 2023. Accessed at https://toronto.citynews.ca/2023/09/15/toronto-public-library-interview-rooms/.
15. Illinois Tech Libraries. "LibGuide: Interview Booth Policies and Rules." May 31, 2023. Accessed at https://guides.library.iit.edu/c.php?g=1154631&p=9231849.
16. Mount Aloysius College. "LibGuide: Career Development: Career Fair Preparation." June 28, 2023. Accessed at https://libguides.mtaloy.edu/c.php?g=691402&p=6593635.
17. Lee, Michelle. "Time to Dress Up: Introducing the NYPL Grow Up Work Fashion Library." *New York Public Library Blogs*, August 6, 2018. Accessed at https://www.nypl.org/blog/2018/08/06/dress-up-nypl-lending-fashion-library.
18. North Carolina State University Libraries. "Making Your Brand: Create Custom Laser-Cut Business Cards." November 3, 2015. Accessed at https://www.denverlibrary.org/ctc/design-your-own-business-cards.
19. Denver Public Library. "Design Your Own Business Cards." 2023. Accessed at https://www.lib.ncsu.edu/events/making-your-brand-create-custom-laser-cut-business-cards.
20. Global News. "Life Skills Classes: The Edmonton Public Library Can Help You Get the Job You Want." November 25, 2022. Accessed at https://globalnews.ca/video/9305220/life-skills-classes-the-edmonton-public-library-can-help-you-get-the-job-you-want/?fbclid=IwAR0I_K-tTafwsY-8k-_SYtO9WQWVhoXodqLvyaqo6Ed-Ol5aBdhX7B8Z664.
21. Bennett, Megan, interview by Madeleine Ildefonso. "Call Number Podcast: Supporting Small Business." *American Libraries*, May 15, 2023. Accessed at https://americanlibrariesmagazine.org/blogs/the-scoop/call-number-podcast-supporting-small-business/.
22. Cleveland Public Library. "Earn the Job, Receive Microsoft Word Certification through Aspire Greater Cleveland." December 14, 2022. Accessed at https://cpl.org/earn-the-job-receive-microsoft-word-certification-through-aspire-greater-cleveland/.

23. ACRL DBIG. "Using Digital Badges to Prepare Students for the University to Workplace Transition." *YouTube Video*, May 3, 2023. Accessed at https://www.youtube.com/watch?v=j05GkAQKx4g.
24. ACT. "ACT WorkKeys National Career Readiness Certificate (NCRC)." Accessed at https://www.act.org/content/act/en/workforce-solutions/act-workkeys/act-workkeys-ncrc.html#eligibility.
25. American Library Association. "ALA Releases Libraries Build Business Communications Toolkit for Library Workers." *ALA News*, May 19, 2023. Accessed at https://www.ala.org/news/press-releases/2023/05/ala-releases-libraries-build-business-communications-toolkit-library-workers.
26. SCNOW. "Lake City Library Conducts Unemployment Benefits Workshop." July 28, 2025. Accessed at https://scnow.com/lifestyles/article_14dc854a-2c04-11e5-b2d9-d3e6e8162685.html.
27. American Bar Association. "What Is 'Expungement'?" *Teaching Legal Docs*, November 20, 2018. Accessed at https://www.americanbar.org/groups/public_education/publications/teaching-legal-docs/what-is-_expungement-/.
28. Hughes, Kathleen, Elena Coelho, and Marshall Shord. "FYI Podcast: Hosting an Expungement Clinic at the Public Library." *Public Libraries Online*, September 26, 2022. Accessed at https://publiclibrariesonline.org/2022/09/new-fyi-podcast-hosting-an-expungement-clinic-at-the-public-library/.
29. Henderson, Andrea Y. "St. Louis County Library Program to Offer Formerly Incarcerated People Business Skills." *St. Louis Public Radio*, May 24, 2023. Accessed at https://news.stlpublicradio.org/economy-business/2023-05-24/st-louis-county-library-program-to-offer-formerly-incarcerated-people-business-skills.
30. Passel, Jeffrey S., and D'vera Cohn. "After Declining Early in the COVID-19 Outbreak, Immigrant Naturalizations in the U.S. Are Rising Again." *Pew Research Center*, December 1, 2022. Accessed at https://www.pewresearch.org/short-reads/2022/12/01/after-declining-early-in-the-covid-19-outbreak-immigrant-naturalizations-in-the-u-s-are-rising-again/.
31. Bennett, Megan, interview by Madeleine Ildefonso. "Call Number Podcast: Supporting Small Business." *American Libraries*, May 15, 2023. Accessed at https://americanlibrariesmagazine.org/blogs/the-scoop/call-number-podcast-supporting-small-business/.
32. Brown, Nicholas. "Three Lessons for Launching Successful Multilingual Programs at Your Library." *OCLC WebJunction*, September 22, 2022. Accessed at https://www.webjunction.org/news/webjunction/launching-successful-multilingual-programs.html.
33. California State Library. "CAreer Pathways Services Locator Map." 2023. Accessed at https://www.library.ca.gov/services/to-public/career-pathways/#map.
34. California State Library. "CAreer Pathways." 2023. Accessed at https://www.library.ca.gov/services/to-public/career-pathways/.
35. California State Library. "Career Online High School." 2023. Accessed at https://www.library.ca.gov/services/to-libraries/career-online-high-school/.
36. San Diego Public Library. "Career Online High School." 2023. Accessed at https://sandiegopl.mycareerhs.com/.
37. Redwood City Public Library. "Job Seekers." 2023. Accessed at https://www.redwoodcity.org/departments/library/services/job-seekers.

2

Specialized Career Services in Libraries

This chapter covers the following:

- Specialized services and support, such as career information literacy
- Lesson plans to teach career development and information literacy in specific areas
- Partnerships and an embedded librarian model for specialized services

When we think about the upcoming changes in workforce development, we see that there is an increasing need to customize how we teach our users to access skills, information, and resources to meet such career needs. In chapter 2, we explore in depth the services and embedded models that might be applicable for your work. We dive into literature and best practices and assignments to showcase what other libraries are doing to promote specialized services and support.

WHAT IS CAREER INFORMATION LITERACY?

Career information literacy is defined as the ability to seek and learn how to find information regarding careers, industries, and companies. A specialized type of information literacy, career information literacy, is knowing where and how to look for career information. Career services professionals in universities are usually tasked with supporting students with this skill development. However, with rapidly changing resources, technologies, and information, librarians can also collaborate and engage with this support. Information literacy in the workplace is common, where workers in any given sector are always seeking information for specific needs.

In *Information Literacy in the Workplace* (2017), Marc Forster writes, the workplace is often a very complex social environment which is focused on the use of information for specific knowledge goals, often with and for the benefits of patients and clients, and often through teams and networks undertaking complex knowledge generating tasks.[1]

It is important to note that any given job could require some information literacy skills, especially for knowledge workers. It is about seeking information, which could be researched in order to "make decisions or influence others in the decision-making process" and may also include utilizing digital technologies for communication skills too.[2] Career information literacy is about all of that plus learning how to identify and research information for career development purposes (see figure 2.1).

Based on this chart, you will see how one should consider developing career information literacy based on utilizing resources and applying them to their own learning purposes or in the workplace.

In addition, there are specific information research instructions depending on the sector or industry. Over time, skills become specialized along with career information literacy; one develops skills, abilities, and knowledge needed to apply what they learn into their workplace successfully or to identify new job opportunities. This chapter covers specific research instructions for various workplaces and career information literacy.

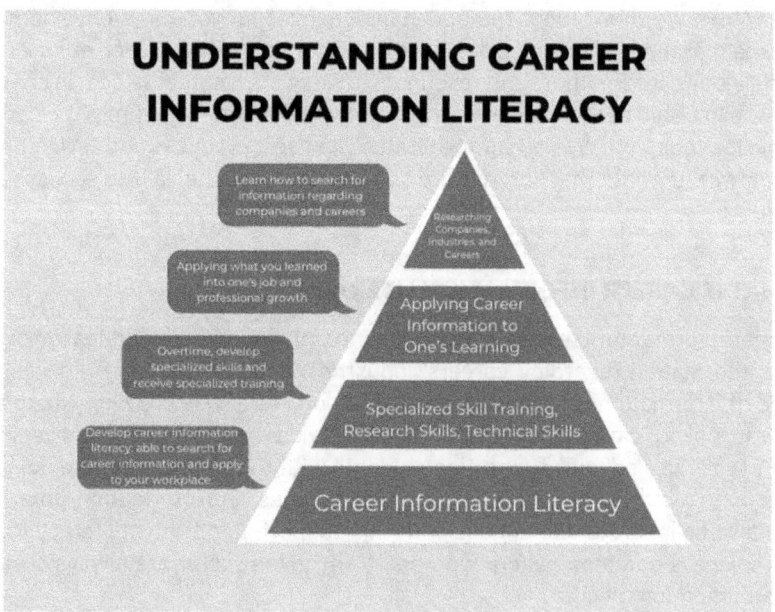

Figure 2.1 Understanding Career Information Literacy in a Hierarchy.
Source: Raymond Pun.

RESEARCH INSTRUCTION, SPECIALIZED TRAINING, AND LESSON PLANS

When we think of specialized skill training and research instruction, library resources can be the best place to start with this type of engagement and support. Here, we will dive into several lesson plans, research instruction programs, and specialized skill training that are focused on career information literacy.

For research instruction in academic libraries, there are two ways to offer this: either embedded in the classroom or as public workshops open to any student/faculty/staff. These lesson plans can be applied to both situations.

For a public workshop, consider the marketing techniques we described in chapter 1 to promote your services to a wider audience on campus or to the general public. You may also consider collaborating with the career services office to ensure that they can promote these services from their department, too. The career services partners can show how to find jobs in specific areas to align with the workshop, and then you as the instructor can teach students how to conduct research on the company, field, or area of interest.

We will explore lesson plans and assignments for you to consider and to modify, according to your own needs. The goal of these short lesson plans is to learn more about your attendees and to engage with their career learning interest through library resources, which may be helpful if you have a LibGuides or some kind of section in your website that highlights these resources for career development. These workshops offer an opportunity to develop library research skills in conjunction with understanding the relevance of library resources for career development.

It is also important to note that certain databases, especially those focused on business, should be used only for academic purposes and not for commercial gains. That condition is dictated by your licensing agreements and terms of service. It is important to remind students that they can use these databases for course work and for their own research. These databases can also support and prepare students for upcoming interviews if they want to know more about the field, industry, and company. For any database you plan to show, it is important to spend time reviewing them and demonstrating the features. These lessons are meant to offer a basic approach to connecting students with specific career interests.

Lesson 1.1: Seeking Information on Arts and Humanities Careers

Objective: Introduce career information opportunities for arts and humanities careers.

Audience: All students majoring or interested in arts and humanities and the general public.

Outcome: To teach relevant resources to develop career information literacy skills and potentially relevant skills for specific careers in arts and humanities.

Working Description: Are you interested in a career in the arts and humanities? Attend this library workshop to learn how library resources can support your career-seeking needs. Knowing library databases can prepare you for a career in the arts and humanities and enable you to impress employers with your research skills and knowledge.

Activity:

- Ask workshop attendees to share what their career interests are and why they are attending the workshop.
- From there, explain which library resources are available for arts and humanities careers. Depending on what your library has access to, you may want to explore some that are subscription-based and some that are open access (which students may continue to use after graduation from your school).
- Spend the first 10 minutes explaining potential careers in the arts and humanities, such as philanthropy, museum work, curatorship, and fundraising/development (for academic librarians, if you partner with career counselors, this part can be shared with them).
- Briefly explain how search terms work, how to use Boolean operators, and how each platform works differently. Give attendees time to explore the databases on their own.

Select Databases and Resources to demonstrate relevant to arts and humanities fields:

- Artstor—a digital library which provides more than 2.5 million images and media files covering the arts, architecture, and humanities with tools for teaching, research, and studying images and visual cultures.
- Candid Learning—a database that offers information for those in nonprofits and those seeking to secure funding and grants. Useful for those interested in development, fundraising, and nonprofit work.
- JSTOR—Search a collection of important scholarly journals representing a range of disciplines.
- MERLOT [Open Access]—The Multimedia Educational Resource for Learning and Online Teaching (MERLOT) system provides access to curated online learning and support materials and content creation tools. MERLOT is led by an international community of educators, learners, and researchers.

- MLA International Bibliography—an online database that contains over 3 million records for those researching modern languages and literature. Useful for those interested in literature and editorial work.
- Proquest Newspapers—an online database that offers searchable cover-to-cover access to historical newspaper content. Generally useful for all doing research on specific companies, industries, and sectors through newspapers.

Lesson 1.2: Seeking Information on Social Sciences Careers

Objective: Introduce career information opportunities for social sciences careers.

Audience: All students majoring or interested in social sciences and the general public.

Outcome: To teach relevant resources to develop career information literacy skills and potentially relevant skills for specific careers in social sciences.

Working Description: Are you interested in a career in the social sciences? Attend this library workshop if you want to learn more about how library resources can support your career-seeking needs. Library databases can prepare you for a career in the social sciences and enable you to impress employers with your research skills and knowledge.

Activity:

- Ask workshop attendees to share what their career interests are and why they are attending the workshop.
- From there, explain which library resources are available for social sciences careers. Depending on what your library has access to, you may want to explore some that are subscription-based and some that are open access (which students may continue to use after they have graduated from your school).
- Spend the first ten minutes explaining such careers in the field of social sciences as nonprofit work, social sciences research, communications, policy, or human resources (If you partner with a career counselor, you can share this part).
- Consider an emphasis on careers in the social sciences focusing on data.
- Briefly show how search terms work, how to use Boolean operators, and how each platform works differently. Give attendees time to explore the databases on their own.

Select Databases and Resources to demonstrate relevant to social sciences fields:

- Data.gov [Open Access]—This database is the U.S. government's open-data website. It provides access to datasets published by agencies across the federal government.
- Ethnic Newswatch—This database covers newspapers, magazines, periodicals, and journals produced by the ethnic and minority press in the United States.
- GenderWatch—This is a full-text database of unique and diverse publications that highlight how gender impacts a variety of subject areas.
- PolicyMap—"An online mapping and GIS tool with data on a wide variety of topics including demographics, real estate, health, jobs, and more."
- APA PsycInfo—From the American Psychological Association, this database contains abstracts of literature in the field of psychology.

Lesson 1.3: Seeking Information on Health Sciences Careers

Objective: Introduce career information opportunities for health sciences careers.

Audience: All students majoring or interested in health sciences and the general public.

Outcome: To teach relevant resources to develop career information literacy skills and potentially relevant skills for specific careers in health sciences.

Working Description: Are you interested in a career in health sciences? Attend this library workshop to learn how library resources can support your career-seeking needs. Library databases can prepare you for a career in the health sciences and impress employers with your research skills and knowledge.

Activity:

- Ask workshop attendees to share what their career interests are and why they are attending the workshop.
- From there, explain which library resources are available for health sciences careers. Depending on what your library has access to, you may want to explore some that are subscription-based and some that are open access (which students may continue to use after they have graduated from your school).
- Spend the first ten minutes explaining such careers in the field of health sciences as medical research, disability services, social work, community health, gerontology, or nonprofit work (academic librarians, who partner with a career counselor can share this part with them).

- Briefly show how search terms work, how to use Boolean operators, and how each platform works differently. Give attendees time to explore the databases on their own.

Select Databases and Resources relevant to health sciences fields:

- PubMed [Open Access]—A free search engine for accessing the MEDLINE database maintained by the National Library of Medicine and the National Institute of Health; the full texts of most articles are accessible.
- MEDLINEPlus [Open Access]—Consumers' health information produced by the National Library of Medicine that is authoritative and up-to-date.
- CINAHL Complete—The definitive research tool for all areas of nursing and allied health literature. It is the most comprehensive source of full text for nursing and allied health journals, providing full text for more than 1,300 journals indexed in CINAHL.
- SPORTDiscus with Full Text—This database covers sport, physical fitness, exercise, sports medicine, sports science, physical education, kinesiology, coaching, training, sport administration, officiating, sport law and legislation, college and university sport, disabled persons, and much more.
- NIMH - Mental Health Topics [Open Access]—Basic information on mental disorders, related topics, and the latest mental health research.

Lesson 1.4a: Seeking Information on Business Careers

Objective: Introduce career information opportunities for business careers.

Audience: All students majoring or interested in business and the general public.

Outcome: To teach relevant resources to develop career information literacy skills and potentially relevant skills for specific careers in business.

Working Description: Are you interested in a career in business? Attend this library workshop if you want to learn more about how library resources can support your career-seeking needs. Knowing library databases can prepare you for a career in business and enable you to impress employers with your research skills and knowledge.

Activity:

- Ask workshop attendees to share what their career interests are and why they are attending the workshop.
- From there, explain what library resources are available for business careers. Depending on what your library has access to, you may want to explore

Specialized Career Services in Libraries

some that are subscription-based and some that are open access (which students may continue to use after they have graduated from your school).
- Spend the first ten minutes explaining such careers in the field of business as marketing, business research, consulting, entrepreneurship, competitive intelligence, finance, and more (for academic librarians, if you partner with a career counselor, share this part with them).
- Briefly how search terms work, using Boolean operators, and how each platform works differently. Give attendees time to explore the databases on their own

Selected databases to demonstrate for industry and company research

- Gale Business Insights—Global company research with detailed profiles including fundamentals, histories, SWOT, investment reports, and market share. Research industries by market share reports and industry rankings. Find business case studies for decision-making strategies. Create comparison charts of companies, countries, and industries.
- Business Source Premier—Full text for more than 2,200 journals, including full text for more than 1,100 peer-reviewed titles in all business disciplines, including marketing, management, MIS, POM, accounting, finance, and economics. Additional full-text, non-journal content includes market research reports, industry reports, country reports, company profiles, and SWOT analyses.
- IBISWorld—A business information database that includes economic, demographic, and government data to provide insight into over 700 industries in America. It includes market conditions and forecasts, supply chain information, risk ratings reports, and business environment profiles.
- Mergent Online—Fully searchable database with financial details of over 13,000 active and inactive public companies listed on the NYSE, AMEX, and NASDAQ exchanges, as well as over 24,000 non-U.S. active and inactive companies. Includes over 300,000 U.S. and international company annual reports.

Lesson 1.4b: Identifying Potential Companies in a Given Industry

Objective: Identifying a list of potential companies in a given industry, especially useful for users who want to identify companies that are hiring or active in industries.

Audience: All students majoring or interested in business and the general public interested in job searching and researching prospective companies.

Outcome: To teach relevant resources to identify potential companies in a given industry.

Working Description: Would you like to know how to find companies in a given sector or field to work in? Learn how to use library databases to conduct company and industry research.

Activity:

- Ask workshop attendees to share what their career interests are or companies they would like to work in; it is also important to determine if the company is public, private, or a subsidiary of a larger parent company.
- From there, explain which library resources are available for finding company and industry information.
- Briefly show how search terms work, how to use Boolean operators, and how each platform works differently. Give attendees time to explore the databases on their own.
- Demonstrate how students can compile a company list through industry search.
  - Explain what industry versus company research means and why they are important for career research.
  - Explain the importance of industry classification codes (e.g., NAICS—North American Industry Classification System): they are part of industry classification systems and there are several systems used by governments and international organizations to collect, synthesize, and analyze specific industries.
  - Show how to access NAICS codes and to search for companies by industry, geography, size, number of employees, and other parameters through business databases.

Select databases and other resources to use to identify companies in specific industries:

- NAICS [https://www.census.gov/naics/]—This official U.S. Government web site provides the latest information on plans for NAICS revisions, as well as access to various NAICS reference files and tools.
- Reference Solutions, from Data Axle (formerly Reference USA) is a business directory that provides information for every open, active business in the United States. Reference Solutions has over 18 million records and is one of the best resources for finding basic information on any operating U.S. business.
- Mergent Online—Fully searchable database with financial details of over 13,000 active and inactive public companies listed on the NYSE, AMEX, and NASDAQ exchanges, as well as over 24,000 non-U.S. active and inactive companies. Includes over 300,000 U.S. and international company annual reports.

Specialized Career Services in Libraries

- Proquest Newspapers—an online database that offers searchable cover-to-cover access to historical newspaper content. Generally useful for all doing research on specific companies, industries, and sectors through newspapers.
- Vault.com—A job-seekers-focused resource that is usually available for free to students. Among the industries covered are consulting, management, law, information technology, and more. Vault provides company profiles and rankings, too.

Lesson 1.4c: Identifying Future Jobs and Trends

Objective: Introduce career information opportunities for future jobs. Jobs are inevitably going to change due to such external forces as generative AI tools, demographics, climate crises, and more.

Audience: All students and the general public.

Outcome: To teach relevant resources for researching future job opportunities and jobs that do not currently exist.

Working Description: Two to five to ten years from now, what kind of jobs will exist? Are you interested in learning how to conduct research on looking at future trends when it comes to job opportunities? This workshop is helpful for those who are uncertain about their career paths or would like to transition to other types of roles that may not exist yet.

Activity:

- Ask workshop attendees to share what industries they are interested in.
- From there, explain which library resources are available for industry research. Depending on what your library has access to, you may want to explore some that are subscription-based and some that are open access (which students will continue to be able to use after they have graduated from your school).
- Explain why future trends and job forecasting is useful (if in partnership with your career center, this role can be delegated to them).
- Briefly show how search terms work, how to use Boolean operators, and how each platform works differently; give attendees time to explore the databases on their own.

Select Databases and Resources to demonstrate for finding employment trends and future jobs:

- U.S. Bureau of Labor Statistics (BLS) [Open Access]—This site contains the most comprehensive stats and other information on cost of labor, minimum wage, employment and unemployment rates, career outlooks and job descriptions, time use surveys ("about the activities people do during the day and how much time they spend doing them"), and more in the United States. There is an "Employment Projections" page that covers information about the labor market for the nation as a whole for 10 years into the future. For example, for 2022-2032, the demand for statisticians, data scientists, and nurse practitioners is expected to grow.
- U.S. Department of Labor: Occupational Employment Statistics (OES) [Open Access]—The OES program provides employment and wage estimates and other information annually for over 800 occupations and across industries.
- Monster.com [Open Access]—A free website that shares posts and information regarding labor statistic and trends related to jobs.
- IBISWorld—This business database offers reports on over 700 U.S. industries providing current trends, statistics, competitors, and a five-year outlook.
- CareerOneStop—Sponsored by the U.S. Department of Labor, Employment and Training Administration, this site provides interview tips, sample resumes and cover letters, and occupation and employment trends.

Lesson 1.4d: Using ChatGPT as a Job Search Tool

Since November 2022, generative AI tools such as ChatGPT have surged into important tools to use in school and in the workplace. Deep concerns about these tools include privacy breaches and ethical considerations (including labor exploitation, replacement of critical thinking, and the potential spreading of mis/disinformation). Companies may be ready to embrace AI and threaten to replace the workforce with this tool. Created by OpenAI, ChatGPT, which includes a free version, is trained on datasets and sources from the Internet to create responses to the user's queries, called prompts. The Urban Library Council released a report in October 2023: "Leadership Brief: Explorations of Generative AI for Library Systems," which explores the impact of AI on jobs, including benefits, risks, and challenges. This report is worth reviewing, though as time passes it may contain increasingly outdated information as generative AI tools rapidly evolve and impact our work.[3]

Generative AI workshops are appearing more in public libraries. The Job & Business Academy at the Queens Public Library held a virtual workshop in August 2023 for the general public called "Incorporating ChatGPT in the Workplace," with the objective of exploring "new ways to use this AI tool to enhance productivity, communication, and problem-solving in the workplace."[4] In November 2023, Topeka & Shawnee County Public Library hosted an AI workshop for the public led by a Microsoft representative, who showed users how to use AI to create cover letters and how to code for a website.[5] The following lesson plan covers ways to use these tools that support one's work in areas such as communication, writing, or coding.

Objective: Introduce how to use generative AI tools such as ChatGPT to research jobs and to prepare for job interviews.

Audience: General public.

Outcome: Learning how to conduct research and prepare for jobs using generative AI tools such as ChatGPT, along with library resources.

Working Description: Interested in learning how tools like ChatGPT can support your job search process? Explore how this new tool can enhance your research and prepare you for job interviews.

Activity:

- Be sure to have a ChatGPT account before you start the program. If you upgrade to ChatGPT 4, you will have access. If you use the free version, you may not have immediate access nor be able to demonstrate in the workshop.
- During the workshop, ask attendees to share which careers, companies, or industries they wish to learn more about.
- Explain what ChatGPT is and show how it works. Interested users will need to create an account to use ChatGPT, at https://chat.openai.com/. Please note the risks of using generative AI tools like ChatGPT, due to past breaches. Users may prefer to create a dummy account or observe how your account works.
- Explain and demonstrate other library resources for job research, such as the databases identified in different lesson plans.
- Show sample prompts on how ChatGPT can help to prepare them for job interviews and for other research. "Prompts" are texts, such as questions or instructions, that you enter into ChatGPT to receive responses.
  - What is important with [insert company/industry/career] that I should be thinking about?
  - I have an interview coming up with [insert company]; what are the biggest opportunities and challenges in [insert company/industry]
    - I have an interview with [insert company] as a [insert role]; what are the most common questions asked in the interview for this role?
    - Generate a list of answers to the questions and provide brief explanations for each answer.

- I am interested in working in/as a [insert career/industry/role]; what training, education, or skills should I consider?
- How can I best demonstrate skills on [insert role]? (You may show a sample job description and paste it in the ChatGPT as a prompt)
- Explain and demonstrate other library resources for job research, such as the databases listed in different lesson plans.

Lesson 1.5: Seeking Information on Science, Technology, Engineering, Agriculture, and Mathematics Careers

Objective: Introduce career information opportunities for sciences, technology, engineering, agriculture, mathematics (STEAM) careers.

Audience: All students majoring or interested in STEAM and the general public.

Outcome: To teach relevant resources to develop career information literacy skills and potentially relevant skills for specific careers in STEAM.

Working Description: Are you interested in a career in STEAM? Attend this library workshop if you want to learn more about how library resources can support your career-seeking needs. Library databases can prepare you for a career in one of the STEAM fields and enable you to impress employers with your research skills and knowledge.

Activity:

- Ask workshop attendees to share what their career interests are and why they are attending the workshop.
- From there, explain which library resources are available for STEAM careers. Depending on what your library has access to, you may want to explore some that are subscription-based and some that are open-access databases for them to develop skills and experience in using it, particularly for students after they graduate from your school.
- Spend the first ten minutes explaining what careers are there in the field of STEAM such as researcher, lab specialist, engineer, consultant, and so forth (for academic libraries, if you partner with a career counselor, this part can be shared by them).
- Briefly explain and show how search terms work, using Boolean operators, and how each platform works differently.
- You can do a quick demonstration on how these tools work and give them time to explore them on their own.

Select Databases and Resources to demonstrate relevant to STEAM fields:

- Agricultural Baseline Database [Open Access]—"The agricultural baseline database provides long run, ten-year projections from USDA's annual long-term projections report."
- Web of Science—This database is an online index that covers journal articles published in the physical and life sciences, health sciences, social sciences, and arts and humanities.
- ArXiv [Open Access]—it is an e-print repository covering physics, mathematics, computer science, nonlinear sciences, quantitative biology, quantitative finance, and statistics.
- Electronic Library of Mathematics (ELibM) contains online journals, article collections, monographs, and other electronic resources in the field of mathematics.
- PLANTS Database [Open Access] provides standardized information about the vascular plants, mosses, liverworts, hornworts, and lichens of the United States and its territories.
- National Sciences Digital Library Funded by the National Science Foundation—most resources linked through here are free. Can be used to find journal articles and has teaching resources.

Lesson 1.6: Seeking Information on Education Careers

Objective: Introduce career information opportunities for education careers.

Audience: All students majored or interested in education and the general public.

Outcome: To teach relevant resources to develop career information literacy skills and potentially relevant skills for specific careers in health sciences.

Working Description: Are you interested in a career in education? Join this library workshop if you want to learn more about how library resources can support your career-seeking needs. Library databases can prepare you for a career in the health sciences and impress employers with your research skills and knowledge.

Activity:

- Ask workshop attendees to share what their career interests are and why they are attending the workshop.
- From there, explain what library resources are available for education careers. Depending on what your library has access to, you may want to explore some that are subscription-based and some that are open-access

databases for them to develop skills and experience in using it, particularly for students after they graduate from your school.
- Spend the first ten minutes explaining what careers are there in the field of education such as educational research, teaching, counselor, academic advisor, and educational technology (for academic libraries, if you partner with a career counselor, this part can be shared by them).
- Briefly explain and show how search terms work, using Boolean operators, and how each platform works differently.
- You can do a quick demonstration on how these tools work and give them time to explore them on their own.

Select Databases and Resources to demonstrate relevant to education field:

- Counseling and Therapy in Video—This resource includes counseling sessions and demonstrations, consultations, lectures, presentations, and interviews. Many of the videos include teaching and discussion guides.
- EdArXiv [Open Access]—An open repository of pre-print (pre-peer reviewed) publications for research in education.
- Education in Video—This resource includes teaching demonstrations, lectures, documentaries, and primary-source footage of students and teachers in the actual classroom.
- Education Source (EBSCO) provides scholarly research and information to meet the needs of education students, professionals, and policymakers. It covers all levels of education as well as all educational specialties like multilingual education, health education, and testing.
- Educational Resources Information Center (ERIC) [Open Access]—an index to educational-related literature. Established in 1966, ERIC is supported by the U.S. Department of Education's Institute of Education Sciences.
- Merlot [Open Access]—The MERLOT system provides access to curated online learning and support materials and content creation tools, led by an international community of educators, learners, and researchers.
- Teaching Channel—This resource offers classroom observations online. Videos that showcase current teaching techniques, model best teaching practices, and provide immediate ideas to support student learning. Includes full, unedited lessons that provide a realistic view of classrooms. Sortable by grade-level (K-12), subject area, and topic.

Lesson 1.7a: Developing Career Research Skills for First-Year Students

Objective: Introduce career information opportunities to first-year students. (This workshop would be general and focused on general career interests and internships since most students in your first year typically do not have a set major or may change their majors.[6])

Audience: First-year students seeking internship or career information.

Outcome: To teach relevant resources to develop career information literacy skills and potentially relevant skills for specific careers.

Working Description: Are you a first-year student seeking an internship or career information? Have you not declared a major yet? Join this library workshop to learn more about how library resources can support your internship/career-seeking needs. We have library databases that can prepare you for careers in many different areas and can impress employers with your research skills and knowledge.

Activity:

- Ask workshop attendees to share what their career interests are and why they are attending the workshop.
- From there, explain what library resources are available for education careers. Depending on what your library has access to, you may want to explore some that are subscription-based and some that are open-access databases for them to develop skills and experience in using it, particularly for students after they graduate from your school.
- Spend the first ten minutes explaining what careers are there based on attendee's interests or broadly explain the career fields from alums (for academic libraries, if you partner with a career counselor, this part can be shared by them).
- Briefly explain and show how search terms work, using Boolean operators, and how each platform works differently.
- You can do a quick demonstration on how these tools work and give them time to explore them on their own.

Select Databases and Resources to demonstrate research skills:

- Career One Stop—Sponsored by the U.S. Department of Labor, Employment and Training Administration, this site provides sample resumes and cover letters, as well as interview tips.
- O*Net Online—The O*NET program is an interactive application for exploring and searching occupations. The database provides the basis for our Career Exploration Tools, a set of valuable assessment instruments for workers and students looking to find or change careers.
- Occupational Outlook Handbook provides recent Bureau of Labor Statistics information about employment in all fields including starting salaries,

educational requirements, and job growth. Excellent resource for career information.
- Data USA—Government data on salaries, job skills, markets, and industries is visually represented using graphs and charts.
- Business Source Premier—Full-text articles from journals and magazines covering business subjects including accounting, finance, economics, marketing, MIS, and operations management, spanning from 1886 to the present.
- Vocational & Career Collection—Vocational & Career Collection is designed for vocational and technical libraries servicing high schools, community colleges, trade institutions, and public libraries. The collection provides full-text coverage for nearly 340 trade and industry-related periodicals.
- Ferguson's Career Guidance Center—Known for its unprecedented depth of coverage, this comprehensive career research database is organized into three main sections: through Industries and Careers, users can explore a multitude of industries, career fields, and professions; Plan Your Education helps users find the schools that fit them best; and Launch Your Career offers solid advice to help users perfect the skills that beget success.

Lesson 1.7b: First-Year Students' Assignment: Seeking New Career Information

Objective: Introduce first-year students to a variety of careers through information seeking.

Audience: First-year students.

Outcome: To teach relevant resources to develop career information literacy skills and potentially relevant skills for specific careers.

Working Description: If you teach a class for first-year students (e.g., first-year seminar or library 101 workshops) or if you are embedded in a course focused on career development or research, you may want to include research instruction focusing on jobs/careers. This assignment may help your students think about library resources and career interests. This can also be a partnership with a course faculty (in any subject) and introduced by the librarian to share how career research and information literacy skills can support their own learning and development.

Activity:

- Introduce the assignment where students
  - Research the career where the interviewee currently based using library databases:

- News Databases:
- Industry Databases:
- Company Databases:
- Students interview the interviewer and ask questions connected to what they found from the databases for interviewer's thoughts
    - Sample Questions:
        - Tell us about your career—how and why did you choose your career?
        - I found _____ in a newspaper database, and I wanted to ask you for your thoughts about it?
        - What are some other similar organizations related to your workplace?
        - I am interested in this career—what should I be considering about this career?
        - If I wanted to research more about the kind of work you do, what would you recommend?
- Students write up a brief reflection about their research experiences, the interview process, and their career goals.

Lesson 1.8: Seeking Graduate School Information Using Library Resources

Objective: Introduce resources to prepare current or former students interested in going to graduate school and teach them how to conduct graduate school research.

Audience: All students or general public interested in attending graduate school.

Outcome: To teach relevant resources to research and review regarding graduate school programs.

Working Description: Interested in learning more about graduate programs? Did you know that the library has many resources to prepare you for graduate school? Learn how these resources can support your graduate school research needs.

Activity:

- Ask workshop attendees to share what their graduate program aspirations are.
- From there, explain what library resources are available for prospective graduate students. Depending on what your library has access to, you may want to explore some that are subscription-based and some that are open-access databases for them to develop skills and experience in using it, particularly for students after they graduate from your school.

- Spend the first ten minutes explaining different types of graduate programs like medical and law schools, and expectations (for academic libraries, if you partner with a career counselor, this part can be shared by them).
- Briefly explain and show how search terms work, using Boolean operators. and how each platform works differently.
- You can do a quick demonstration on how these tools work and give them time to explore them on their own.

Select Databases and Resources to demonstrate research skills:

- Law school or legal research: LexisNexis Academic provides access to full-text news, business, and legal publications, using a variety of flexible search options. Access includes over 10,000 news, business, and legal sources. Your local public law library may have other databases available to explore on-site.
- Medical school programs or health-related fields—PubMed [Open Access]—A free search engine for accessing the MEDLINE database maintained by the National Library of Medicine and the National Institute of Health, most articles have a full text that you must link out to a publisher site.
- Business school programs—there are business databases available in your local library that you may want to explore remotely or on-site. You may want to also consider newspaper databases to look up company news and what is covered about specific industries. For small businesses, check out SCORE [open access] and Small Business Administration [open access] for information about free business education and resources and funding.
- Higher education—*The Chronicle of Higher Education* covers all topics related to the academic workplace; it is a resource to identify potential schools, jobs, and other academic program information. In addition, check out Project Muse to read the latest peer-reviewed articles and monographs across academic disciplines.
- Proquest Dissertation and Theses is also a useful resource to identify the latest research and published dissertations and theses by graduate students and explore new topics and advisors that they have worked with.

Lesson 1.9: Seeking Information on Vocational and Technical Careers

Academic careers or careers that require a college degree are not always for everyone. Opportunities to engage with nonacademic, technical, and vocational careers are areas to consider. There may be folks who do have college degrees and may want to pursue vocational and technical careers, and this is where you may want to inform them of the library resources. We define vocational careers as specific jobs, trade, or fields such as carpentry, paralegal, electrician, plumber, and cosmetology.

Objective: Introduce users on what vocational careers are available and how library resources can prepare them.

Audience: General public.

Outcome: To teach relevant resources to research and prepare for vocational careers.

Working Description: Are you interested in exploring careers such as carpentry, paralegal, electrician, plumber, and cosmetology? Library resources can support your career research and training in these areas and more. This workshop will cover library resources to support vocational and technical career pathways.

Activity:

- Ask workshop attendees to share what their career interests are.
- From there, explain what library resources are available for them. Depending on what your library has access to, you may want to explore some that are subscription-based and some that are open-access databases for them to develop skills and experience in using it, particularly for students after they graduate from your school.
- Spend the first ten minutes explaining different types of vocational careers and expectations including certifications (for academic libraries, if you partner with a career counselor, this part can be shared by them). You may want to explain the importance relevance of trade associations in these vocational careers for information and networking purposes.
- Briefly explain and show how search terms work, using Boolean operators and how each platform works differently.
- You can do a quick demonstration on how these tools work and give them time to explore them on their own.

Select Databases and Resources to research or prepare for vocational and trade careers:

- Vault.com [Open access]—A free resource focusing on various industries that are for job seekers. The industry includes consulting, management, law, information technology, and more. They provide company profiles and rankings too.

- GlobalEdge Industry Profiles [Open Access]—from Michigan State University, this free resource provides an overview of several industries including relevant links to industry associations and risks related to the industry.
- Small Business Administration [Open Access]—This resource from the U.S. Small Business Administration provides resources for people interested in starting their own business and includes business plan templates and information on grants.
- Proquest Newspapers—An online database that offers searchable cover-to-cover access to historical newspaper content. Generally useful for all doing research on specific companies, industries, and sectors through newspapers.
- Mometrix—A database that offers access to test preparation materials for over 1,000 different standardized and certification exams.

Embedded Model and Liaison Librarianship: Partnerships

When you are planning to reach out to specific groups, it is best to partner with agencies or social services that may already be outreaching or connected to such groups, especially for those in a public library. For academic and school libraries, you may consider partnering with career centers or student affairs/services programs to meet these specific groups. In this part of the section, we will dive into ways to partner with such groups and how to engage and support these specific groups. First, let us define what these types of collaborative support mean.

Embedded Model—Barbara A. Alvarez, author of *Embedded Business Librarianship for the Public Librarian* (2016) writes, "the overall goal for this [embedded librarian] position is a consistent focus on learning and understanding the business community on a meaningful level, as well as positioning the library as an organization that is part of the business community."[7] As a librarian, we need to become embedded in the community and engage with these community members by attending meetings, initiating programming, or sharing information/resources from the library. Being an embedded librarian means building and cultivating relationships with our users and maintaining connections through mutual shared interest. You learn more about your users and their issues and experiences whether that is starting a business, applying for a job, finding statistics about specific industries, or identifying grad programs. These are touch points where the library/embedded librarian can support and identify resources, positioning the library as an important member of the community. Afterall, librarianship work is relationship-centered work. How do you start to become an embedded librarian and form partnerships? The partnership section goes a bit deeper in different areas for you to consider.

Liaison Librarianship—Based on subject librarians' role in academic libraries, there is a role for liaison librarians to be embedded in different departments and schools in the university like Career Center, Student Affairs, and Business

Schools. Liaison librarians may have content expertise or subject knowledge and functional expertise. They interact with their liaisons and support programmatic efforts through collections and services, and what the library can offer, as a partner in other ways.

Although it is important to note the criticism of liaison librarianship because there are ongoing demands in the position, a lack of clarity at times. Narlock and Robinson writes,

> besides expanding subject librarians' roles, many academic libraries have also responded by creating a new kind of liaison: the functional specialist, whose expertise is not in subject content but rather in tools, methods and practical domains that matter to our patrons. Example areas of functional specialization include text mining and analysis, geographic information systems (GIS) software, data visualization, and copyright law.[8]

The challenge of being a liaison is that you often have to stay updated and informed about trends, technologies, and resources. It is still important to build and maintain relationships through liaison librarianship and partnership.

Partnerships and Referral Relationships

Generally, you/library should always strive to be the "connector." The library is always striving to partner and connect users with specific resources and needs. The goal of libraries is to build relationships by focusing on your users' needs through partnerships and to develop an engaged network that can support your community of users.

How do you start your partnerships? Like any project that requires multiple stakeholders, you will need to communicate and engage with others for support and feedback. Librarian Fannie M. Cox writes that

> collaboration is an important learned behavior. Librarians have long understood the importance of relationship building due to their long history of providing programming, working with communities they serve and support, and building cooperative relationships amongst each other . . . The goal is to provide and bridge relationships to form social networks that not only strengthens our society, but enhances quality of life and improves communities.[9]

In this context, we focus on the job development opportunities that libraries can bring forward to their communities by identifying existing partnerships, referral relationships, and collaborating and sharing resources, especially wraparound services, especially those with other needs.

Here are various partners to consider in your community:

Community and Local Groups—Have you looked at your community groups that might be supportive of your workforce development initiatives/programs? This could be Rotary Club, YWCA Services, or groups that members of your Friends of the Library are part of. Meetup is a resourceful website to identify groups in the areas to partner with. It is also important to consider "national organizations" that might have a "chapter" or regional hub in your area where you can connect. This could be a great opportunity to learn what job seekers in such groups may be looking for or what skills they would like to develop that the library can support.

The U.S. Chamber of Commerce—It is a nonprofit connected to business organizations and brings together a group of businesses that supports their members. You may want to attend their meetings or meet with the leadership individually to learn more about their work and ways for your library to partner with them. This could be a great opportunity to learn what job requirements or skill demands they are looking for in terms of job candidates and for the library to prepare community members for such roles. Start at https://www.uschamber.com/co/chambers

Workforce Agencies or Centers like Career One Stop or State Government Departments of Labor or Employment (in the United States) are likely the most relevant local partner organizations for your programs because their goal is to support job seekers with job opportunities through skill training and networking. This is not to say that the library's program will replace their services but to overlap and optimize such services. Consider the SWOT Analysis Chart below to ask yourselves questions about such partnerships. Start at https://www.dol.gov/agencies/whd/state/contacts

Trade and Professional Associations—There are many trade or professional associations out there. We discussed how to search for them in chapter 1, and you might want to consider doing extensive research on which groups might be a good partner with your library. Trade or Professional Associations usually have their chapter/regional hubs so you can connect locally with them. It is a great way to learn what some of the members of these groups are searching for, in terms of skill development/training or jobs.

You can also use the Gale Directory Library Database if your library subscribes to it. Gale Directory Library Database contains directories on companies, publishers, associations, and more, which may provide statistics on specific industries too. If your library does not subscribe to it, you can also search for associations online, via Google, using the following techniques and examples:

- site:*.org and nursing association
- site:help engineers association

Higher Education, Universities, and Colleges—Locally, there are universities, colleges, and community colleges to consider partnering with. The best approach is the career center because that is the way to align services and resources and support one another. Every university has a career center, and you can reach out to see if there is interest in partnership. It is likely easier if you are an academic librarian in the same institution but if you are a public librarian, it may require meetings or connections because career centers are often strapped with limited time and resources and need to prioritize their services to the academic community. It can also be an information-sharing partnership.

For example, if you have an upcoming program or job fair focused on immigrant students or veteran students, you can share this with the career center and they will share it with the appropriate partners. Career Centers today are envisioning ways to create more community and skill development projects that may lead to new job opportunities. This may be an opening opportunity for the public library to engage with higher education while connecting on the careers and skills that academic programs are preparing students for.

Community outreach and partnerships for academic libraries/higher education are often included in the mission or strategic priorities whether that is through their service learning programs, community services, or fostering better alignment with community interest. Librarian Fannie Cox writes,

> For academic libraries, the term "community" has broadened to include not only students, faculty, and staff, who are the internal members of the academic community of the institution but also the neighboring communities that surround the physical space of the library setting.[10]

California State University, Fresno Library partnered with the Fresno County Public Library to offer technology services and workshops to the community. Funded by a community grant, this collaboration enabled student ambassadors to teach technology workshops on how to write a resume or cover letter, how to use the Internet, and how to code in different languages such as Spanish, Hmong, Arabic, and Hindi. This short-term project enabled professional growth for undergraduate student ambassadors, a key partnership between two institutions, and supported the needs of job seekers in Fresno, California.[11]

Of course, any partnership can take time to develop or can stymie or misdirect your priorities. It is always best to gather information, ask questions, and create a common language for terms of agreements. You may also want to ask yourselves these questions when thinking about forming partnerships with groups listed above (see Table 2.1).

These sample questions are meant to guide you and your team's thinking when approaching a partner organization for this program. Even when these

Table 2.1 A SWOT Analysis Chart. Question: What are the Opportunities and Challenges for Partnerships?

Strengths	Weaknesses
• What are the advantages of this partnership? • How does this partnership foster or increase presence and engagements for your targeted group? • What strengths do you and your partner organizations bring?	• What is the weakness of this partner organization? (e.g., lack of staff, unresponsiveness, and lack of resources) • What gaps do you and your partner organizations have? • What resources are missing in this partnership?

Opportunities	Threats
• What unique opportunities does this partnership bring that you/library cannot do alone? • What are your strengths that can turn into opportunities? • Are there opportunities to continue this partnership?	• What challenges this partnership? • What if this partnership takes up more time and capacity from your/team? • How do you balance your priorities?

partnerships do not work out as intended or do not sustain over time, you have succeeded in introducing the library and its services and resources to constituents that may not have realized the extensive offerings.

Wraparound Services—When thinking about the circumstances of your users, wraparound services may be the method to bridge critical resources and services to support their needs when searching for a job. "Wraparound shifts focus away from a traditional service-driven, problem-based approach to care and instead follows a strengths-based, needs-driven approach. The intent is to build on individual and family strengths to help families achieve positive goals and improve well-being."[12] Users may need services such as child care, food assistance, or medical assistance. In your role, you may help identify such resources and refer your users to specific services and partners. A library's career services building partnerships with a variety of social services and programs may help fully engage with users and address barriers impacting their job searching process. The Public Library Association's recorded webinar called, "Partnering to Meet Community Workforce Needs" on August 19, 2021, offered tons of information and examples of how public libraries form partnerships. The website also offered slide deck and resources for you to explore.[13]

For academic libraries, an exploratory study found that the proximity of the locations between the business libraries and career services are likely to foster collaboration naturally. In this qualitative study, Pun found that academic libraries that are situated near career centers on campus or share the same building are likely to form partnerships or there may be growth for collaboration between the two. "One participant noted that once the career center moved to another location, it created a gap in their partnership. Sharing the same building tends to generate opportunities to collaborate."[14] A shared space or close proximity may help cultivate partnerships. Since this is not the case for many libraries, it is important to have a dedicated liaison who can directly connect and do outreach with career services, to joint-host workshops, share information, and build rapport. With overlapping interest in supporting student success, career services is a natural partner for academic libraries.

Specific Groups and Demographics to Consider:

When thinking about specific groups to serve, you will have to customize your programs and services to meet their needs. Here are some groups and ways to engage and support their job-seeking needs.

Rural Communities—Workforce development programs through collaborations can greatly support rural communities. Rural communities also face different challenges compared to urban or suburban settings such as broadband access. How would you engage with rural communities scattered across an area? Consider exploring associations and groups like the Association for Rural & Small Libraries [https://www.arsl.org/], Association of Bookmobile and Outreach Services [https://abos-outreach.com/], or The Rural Library Network [https://partnersrural.org/]. Each of these groups can share best practices and ideas for libraries to engage with communities in rural settings. For example, the Rural Library Network provides resources and connections on workforce programming and community engagement.

The Rural Library Network hosted the Rural Summit: From Cradle to Career to

> bring together teachers, principals, superintendents, higher education leaders, legislators, and nonprofit leaders to share ideas and strategies for ensuring that rural youth have the opportunity to enter school ready to learn and successfully transition from high school to college and career.[15]

In addition, they have a unique example called, "The Appalachian Cradle-to-Career Partnership," which "aims to create generational success and transform the regional economy. We are a coalition of partners supporting youth and families in Kentucky's Promise Zone, ensuring equitable life outcomes from cradle to career."[16] In this partnership program, there were skill-building workshops, college and career learning for families, and secured funding from numerous community groups and foundations, which will support students developing academic skills in literacy and math, and be on a path to employment.

Collaborations can also take place between academic and public libraries. For example, in 2021, the Wyoming Library to Business (WL2B) "connects Wyoming entrepreneurs and business owners with a curated network of business experts, resources to learn new skills, and the tools to succeed at every stage. It is business-focused, community-driven, and a completely free resource to Wyoming citizens."[17] The partnerships formed among Wyoming State Library, the Campbell County Public Library, the Natrona County Library, the Laramie County Public Library, and the University of Wyoming Libraries supported Wyoming entrepreneurs and small business owners through information services and support and offered studio spaces for video production to expand pitches, marketing, and advertising work. Collaboration between two different libraries requires training and outreach.

Veterans—According to the Census Bureau's American Community Survey (2021), which includes annual estimates of veterans, there are over 16 million veterans in the United States.[18] Many libraries have created a "Veterans Center" as a way to share resources and information with veteran users. The California State Library has a "Veterans Connect: Resources for Serving Veterans," where there are training resources, mental health programs, and other pertinent information to veterans. Partnering with your State Library, State Government or local groups focused on veterans' interest is a good way to build rapport and to share library resources on workforce development.

Authors Sarah LeMire and Kristen J. Mulvihill of *Serving Those Who Served: Librarian's Guide to Working with Veteran and Military Communities* (2017) writes,

> Because the military is the first and only job held by many service members, they may be unfamiliar with even the basics of the civilian job hunt. Although the military's programs for transitioning veterans include information about resume development and job-hunting strategies, the transition period is so stressful and busy that separating service members may not fully absorb this advice.[19]

LeMire and Mulvhill also recommend libraries to offer workshops specifically for veterans on finding and applying for jobs and interviewing strategies. Public Libraries can partner with state veterans' associations focused on veteran employment interests. For academic libraries, librarians can partner with career centers and the veterans services center on campus to connect and engage with this specific group. Librarians can offer personalized workshops and consultation to veterans or collaborate with community based partners to host job fairs specifically for veterans if there is a need or growing population in your community.

People Who Are Unhoused—According to the Department of Housing and Urban Development Annual Homelessness Assessment Report, "in 2023, they found nearly 600,000 Americans are unhoused on any night."[20] People who are unhoused face stigmatization and many other factors that prevent them from applying for a job. In addition, they may be experiencing other types of hardships that are visible or invisible to you. Most jobs require a permanent address, and it becomes difficult for people who are unhoused to secure a steady job.

Libraries can partner with social services from the community, recruit a social worker in the library, and create a programmatic effort to support this community of users addressing the barriers and needs that they may encounter or have. The Orange County Public Library and in partnership with the Orange County Housing Authority offered "Housing Choice Voucher Program" and residents can apply for rental assistance. Paper applications and in-person assistance are available across the libraries of Orange County, California.[21]

Ryan Dowd, author of *The Librarian's Guide to Homelessness An Empathy-driven Approach to Solving Problems, Preventing Conflict, and Serving Everyone* (2017), writes that libraries can be of help to homeless individuals: employment and email. People who are unhoused do not own or have immediate access to computers. To apply for jobs, you often need an email address and access to a computer and Internet. The library can offer email and set up workshops for job search purposes, and it might be one way to support people who are unhoused searching for employment. Most importantly, Dowd calls on library workers to treat people who are unhoused with respect, dignity, and humanity, recognizing their existence with kindness and by actively listening to their needs. It is important to build rapport with community members through the existing library's resources, services, and referrals to other social services.

Immigrants and Refugees—The United Nations Refugee Agency (UNHCR) and the World Bank recently shared estimated data regarding the number of refugees globally: the number "rose to 35.3 million in 2022, a steep increase from 27.1 million in 2021."[22] As a result, libraries need to identify ways to actively support such communities of users who are looking for job opportunities. In the United States, libraries can provide access to legal documents such as I-765, an application for employment authorization, and application assistance programs to prepare them for employment opportunities. Signage needs to be translated into appropriate languages for users to see. It must be clear that the library staff should not help users fill out the form. Legal documents require users to fill them out in a timely fashion. If you are unsure, you can direct them to legal consultations such as the directory of "Recognized Organizations and Accredited Representatives Roster by State and City" from the Department of Justice or IMMI, an immigrant online resources tool.[23]

In Wisconsin, the Madison Public Library partners with groups such as Centro Hispano–Immigrant services as an e-resource which is available to all library users. "Centro Hispano offers immigration services including consultations, naturalization, permanent residence, DACA, and family assistance. Visit the website for times and to make an appointment. This service has a minimum cost."[24] Forming partnerships with local groups can help your communities and your libraries through the referral process.

In addition to providing paperwork, there are other factors to meet the needs of job seekers who are immigrants such as language training and meeting jobs in demand. In New York, the Queens Public Library (QPL), Fatma Ghailan, Assistant Director, writes that "we offer several English-language programs targeted to both general audience and prospective employees. Two of our Learn English for Work, administered through the e-learning platform Voxy EnGen, specifically focuses on English for career paths in healthcare and technology."[25] QPL works with case managers and receives funding from the U.S. Department of Labor to provide support with documentation and job search and interview preparedness. "[This work] requires investing in strong partnerships between our libraries and the communities we serve to create a talent pipeline between immigrants and local employers."[26]

In the United Kingdom, Ukrainian refugees have sought support from the Devon Libraries. "Throughout the last year or so our libraries have helped many new arrivals from Ukraine with everything from Ukrainian language books to support accessing services online and connecting with their local community." These services offer incredible ways for immigrants, migrants, and refugees to stay engaged in the community.[27] With increasing migrants and refugees, identifying connections through resources is key in ensuring that they feel welcomed in the library space.

In Canada, the Library Settlement Partnerships (LSP) is a program for those who are new to Canada to speak with a settlement worker for information on housing, employment, language learning resources, education, and more. Sponsored by the Government of Canada,

> The Library Settlement Partnerships (LSP) offers a unique and innovative newcomer information service in 11 communities throughout Ontario. This service includes one-on-one settlement information and referrals, group information sessions, and community outreach. Over 60 newcomer settlement workers from 23 agencies work out of the 49 branches of 11 public libraries in communities with high newcomer populations. Services are provided in a variety of languages, based on community needs.[28]

This kind of program can be hosted in your library and in partnerships with local groups and immigrant service agencies. When engaging with immigrants who speak another language, recognize the barriers and limitations that they may encounter in the workforce and workplace.

Reentry/Transition to the Community For Formerly Incarcerated—The Prison Policy Initiative, a nonprofit public policy think tank focused on criminal justice matters shared in 2018, "using a nationally representative dataset, we provide the first ever estimate of unemployment among the five million formerly incarcerated people living in the United States."[29] People who were formerly incarcerated and now in reentry/transition mode will experience a number of hurdles in applying for jobs due to their record. We talked about expungement clinics in your library in chapter 1 that some libraries are doing that you may refer to. There have also been dedicated career navigators who are specialists who can connect and support learners to explore career options and identify appropriate skills and education, and resources needed for them, and can meet with users and refer to appropriate resources. Before applying for jobs, people may experience other barriers such as housing, financial set up, technology access, and so forth.

In May 2023, Nazish Dholakia, a senior writer at the Vera Institute of Justice, an independent nonprofit national research and policy organization in the United States, describes how partnerships support job seekers who have been incarcerated before:

> for more than 600,000 people leaving prison every year, these training programs can significantly reduce barriers to employment—and that benefits them and their families. It's also a win for employers, who seek skilled workers and are increasingly relying on this largely untapped labor pool.[30]

In a nationwide study, the Institute for Justice found that people with criminal records experience severe occupational licensing barriers and could hamper their opportunities for successful reentry to society.[31] It is important to understand how your services to these groups may be impacted based on policies and laws embedded in your state.

Dr. Jeanie Austin, author of *Library services and incarceration: Recognizing barriers, Strengthening Access* (2021) shares that "the San Diego County Library provided month long trainings on employment and job-seeking, and coordinated connections to library resources through outreach to Parole and Community Team (PACT) meetings (meetings that people who are paroled from California prisons must attend)."[32] The Career High School Online is one important resource to support those in this group. GED preparation programs and life skill training could be programs that the library offers.

Dr. Taffany Lim, Executive Director of Engagement, Service, and the Public Good in the California State University, Los Angeles, and co-founder of the "Prison BA Initiative," which is "the only face to face bachelors degree completion program for incarcerated students in the state of California,"[33] shares that many formerly incarcerated students often face technology challenges such as applying for jobs online, turning documents into PDF, and using Google Docs. In a conversation, Dr. Lim also described that those who are formerly incarcerated may not know how to apply for driver's license or access social security or birth certificates information.

One recommendation is to consider a referral system within the library to ensure that there are key partnerships with specific agencies and resources to share out and support these needs. "Connected to a school is to their advantage, libraries can refer to local community colleges, high school diploma programs, GED preparations, certificates and vocational training programs" as Dr. Lim explained. Organizations like Center for Employment Opportunities (CEO),

> works to reduce recidivism and increase employment. [CEO] provides people returning from prison immediate paid employment, skills training, and ongoing career support. To offer work experience, CEO operates transitional work crews that provide supplemental indoor/outdoor maintenance and neighborhood beautification services to more than 40 customers across the U.S.

Referrals for those who are formerly incarcerated to such programs may be greatly beneficial and may address job applying barriers.

In one example, in Georgia, the Gwinnett County Public Library (GCPL) created the "New Start Entrepreneurship Incubator" (NSEI) in 2021 and offered a six-month course supporting community members who have been incarcerated to start and build their own businesses. NSEI was funded by Google and in partnership with the ALA's national Libraries Build Business Initiative. About fifteen to twenty participants attended monthly meetings and presentations by local business owners and experts focusing on topics such as marketing, financial management, and writing a business plan. The library provided laptops and WiFi hotspots for those in the program, and participants completed online course work and received mentorship. In addition, Duffie Dixon, director of marketing and communications at GCPL shared, "participants [received] an opportunity to pitch their business proposals to a Shark Tank–style panel of judges to receive feedback and potentially obtain start-up capital."[34] These activities can be fostered for this group but partnership is key to secure funding, program development, and coordination.

People with Disabilities—This group of job seekers may encounter challenges in the job search process. According to the U.S. Census Bureau data from 2021, there are about "42.5 million Americans with disabilities, making up 13% of the civilian noninstitutionalized population."[35] The disabilities may also be visible or invisible. It is important to consider and address the biases that we may hold or within our institutions.

Northwestern Polytechnic Library, a college in Alberta, Canada, created a research guide called, "Career Hub for Job Seekers."

This hub will help you explore career options by identifying your skills, getting information about the [labor] market, and researching related programs. It will also help you with the process of applying for jobs, including creating a resume and cover letter.[36]

One section focuses on job seekers with disabilities and highlights how job seekers can prepare their job search process through arranging for accommodations as well as disclosing a disability and how to and when to disclose. The types of suggestions shared in this research guide can also become a template on how you may host workshops catered to employers who are seeking to recruit people with disabilities and what they should know about.

In Toronto Public Library, librarians organized a job fair for people on the autism spectrum. Planning for months, the librarians spoke with job seekers on the spectrum on what they wanted a job fair to be like. The job fair was designed for neurodiverse people. For example, participants wore a communication badge indicating the type of social interactions that they prefer to have. "People on the spectrum face high levels of unemployment and barriers to participation in Canada, and Toronto's libraries want to help make their spaces more inclusive."[37] The organizers also partnered with social workers and consultants to put the program together. This example demonstrates how librarians should always center the people in mind and have conversations while planning for such an event or program.

Like the other groups, outreach through partnership is key to get the word out to introduce how libraries can support job seekers who are disabled such as workshops on researching organizations and workplaces that offer accommodations and identifying ways to advocate for such accommodations too. Referral to specific groups to support advocacy work is an important consideration. There may be organizations dedicated to supporting the community of job seekers who are disabled. For example, Life Works, a nonprofit group based in Minnesota, "partners with people with disabilities to drive change by increasing opportunity and access in the community"[38] can offer tremendous resources and support by matching people with disabilities with appropriate work opportunities. Identifying these referrals and establishing connections with agencies supporting disabled workers can be a helpful resource.

Small Business Owners—There are over 32 million small businesses in the United States according to the Small Business Administration. The U.S. federal government defines "small business" as one with as many as 499 employees. Many small businesses have limited resources and may rely on public resources from the library. Consider identifying small business groups through the Chamber of Commerce The Small Business Administration page is also a great resource to support entrepreneurs on business startup plans, templates, and information on grants.

Workshops for this group may include the following:

- Finding Grants as a Small Business Owner and Entrepreneur: How to identify, research, and write grant proposals for small business development and entrepreneurship program.
- Learn how to research and obtain basic patents to protect you from intellectual property theft:[39] Do you have creators who would like to patent their work or obtain copyright training? This workshop focuses on how to research patents using library, commercial, or government databases such as Patent Public Search, Google Patents, or Scopus.
- Conducting market research and researching competitions: Introduce library resources and government databases (see below) on how to conduct market research in different industries and ways to identify competitors in the same industry.
- Learning how to use databases like Gale's Small Business Resources to conduct research and identify resources.[40]
- Resources to Explore:
  - Small Business Administration (SBA): From the U.S. Small Business Administration, this site contains many useful information from loan information to business plan development templates. SBA can be very resourceful to those starting small businesses. [https://www.sba.gov/]
  - SCORE, "Counselor to America's Small Business": Another useful resource for small business owners and entrepreneurs, SCORE, offers live workshops, mentorship, and connections to networks. [https://www.score.org/]

    BRASS Business Guide on Small Business & Entrepreneurship: From the American Library Association's Business References and Services Association (BRASS),

  - This [free] guide covers aspects of small business and entrepreneurship information that are most commonly sought after by library patrons. This includes, but is not limited to the following: how to start a small business, business forms, franchising information, acquiring funding, and business plans."[41]
  - The NYPL's Small Business Resource Center: A useful website from NYPL containing business development plans and resources. Even if you do not live in New York City, the information here might be helpful to support your community of small business owners and entrepreneurs.[42] [https://brass.libguides.com/SmallBusinessCore]
  - Balance Building Your Business: [https://www.nypl.org/help/services/smallbiz]

In addition, you may consider creating a formal community learning program, where participants can sign up to learn and learn in person in the library

Specialized Career Services in Libraries

or online like the Entrepreneur Academy. In Maryland, the Enoch Pratt Free Library in partnership with Baltimore County Public Library (made possible by Urban Libraries Council) offered the Entrepreneur, an innovative community program providing access to training for small business entrepreneurs and solopreneurs. Participants would learn:

- Marketing research and business strategies
- Ask the experts panel
- Financing options
- Financial recordkeeping and taxes
- Marketing your business
- Developing your business plan[43]

On March 30, 2023, the Queens Public Library organized a "Business Resources Day" from 3 to 5 pm in one of their branch libraries. They invited representatives from Queens Chamber of Commerce and city agencies to share information to attendees interested in small business development. When you offer these events focused on specific groups and in partnerships with others, it is likely to garner attention and interest. "The Queens Chamber of Commerce and the office of Council Member Linda Lee are hosting a multilingual Small Business Resource Fair. business owners will have the opportunity to meet and greet representatives from city agencies and local organizations."[44]

It is also important to note that minority owned businesses such as those by women and people of color tend to experience different challenges when trying to secure a loan from a bank due to a variety of reasons such as not having a commercial account with a bank and so forth. According to Luz Urrutia of the Accion Opportunity Fund,

> We're seeing a lot of women starting new business[es] and in particular women of color ... But that's not necessarily a positive thing. A lot of folks have been laid off or because their financial situation means they have to start a side business to support their family.[45]

As reported by the Kauffman Foundation, a nonprofit that bolsters entrepreneurship, roughly 30 percent of new entrepreneurs in 2020 were unemployed.[46] Another consideration for a rise of entrepreneurship is the traditional workplace cultures. Toxic workplaces have been a major factor that cause people to rethink their options and opportunities as described by a report by *MIT Sloan Management Review* analyzing over 34 million online employee profiles.[47] Developing and marketing programming to support entrepreneurs and community members in job transition due to a variety of reasons is the best investment for libraries to commit to.

INTERVIEWS AND PROFILES

In this section, we will highlight librarians supporting instructional services and programming in career services and career information literacy. Real case studies are offered to provide context on the work of others. We speak with librarians Kara Van Abel, Monika Chavez, and Rebecca Hastie to hear their thoughts on supporting career development, job seekers, and business students.

An Interview with Kara Van Abel, Associate Professor, Reference Librarian and Liaison to the Collat School of Business at the University of Alabama at Birmingham

Question 1: Can you tell us a bit about your role? How did you come up with the idea to start the Business Research Toolkit?
Kara: As the liaison to the business school, I am responsible for ensuring that faculty, students, and staff know about the resources the library offers. My day-to-day is spent helping facilitate projects between the business school and the libraries and providing reference instruction on an as-needed basis. In addition to the toolkit course, I also teach several one-shot sessions for a variety of classes and serve as the academic integrity coordinator for the libraries. The original toolkit creator, Jeff Graveline, set out to build a course that would cover core business information skills useful in both the classroom and professional environment. When I started at UAB in 2016, the toolkit was well established; however, it was taught during the business day in a face-to-face format that didn't fully meet the needs of students. The course received a full overhaul back in 2017, when it was moved to an online format in our learning management system. It's much more robust now, and we get participants from disciplines all across campus representing UAB students, staff, and even faculty.

Question 2: You have had over 1,000 recipients since starting this program in 2010, congratulations! How has the program changed since? Or if it has not changed, what and how would you like to do differently with it if you had more time/resources?
Kara: As I mentioned, the toolkit was overhauled in 2017 when it was moved online. The core concept of the course is the same. It was originally designed to cover specific areas of business research including: the research process, company research, industry research, advanced search strategies, demographics and business statistics, and international research. There are also elective modules like basic patent searching and career research. Those are both new, and the asynchronous, online format allows any UAB faculty, staff, or student to complete the toolkit no matter their schedule. Additionally, in the spring of 2023, a digital badging pathway was created so that participants who

successfully complete the toolkit can link digital badges to their social media platforms and online portfolios. Digital badging also allows for the toolkit modules to be embedded in courses at the business school in a standalone format. This is an exciting new development that I hope will open the door to more students completing the full certificate course.

The possibilities for the toolkit are endless, and it's always evolving according to student needs. I'm certain there is not a single thing in the course that hasn't been added or updated in the past few years. I'm currently in the process of building a new elective module with the help of our media literacy librarian, Brooke Becker, to help students evaluate potential sources more effectively.

Question 3: Do you/library have any partnerships with your career services center at University of Alabama at Birmingham? If so, can you talk a bit about it? If not, what are your thoughts on academic libraries partnering with career services centers to support business research skills for career development?

Kara: I don't work directly with our office of career services, but several of their staff members have taken the Business Research Toolkit course and earned the certificate. I have a career research module in my toolkit, and it actually covers some of the same tools their office promotes. Although, the career service office offers much more in-depth coverage than I can in my elective module. I do include suggestions for certificate recipients on ways to add the toolkit to their resumes, and the digital badge also makes it easier for potential employers to understand what the certificate is and the skills that it covers. This is sparking some ideas for ways to work with them to get more participation in my toolkit course and also promote their services more among students! I'm always thinking about how to leverage partnerships and improve visibility for our resources.

Question 4: What are key resources you recommend for librarians interested in teaching business information literacy?

Kara: Business information literacy has many components, and there are so many great resources to help someone getting started. Celia Ross' book, *Making Sense of Business Reference*, which was updated in 2019 is a great primer, and I always suggest that to any new business librarian I meet. She also teaches a course, Business Reference 101, periodically through RUSA and that's a great introduction to business reference resources. The Business Reference Competencies, published by RUSA BRASS and also endorsed by the Special Library Association, Business & Finance Division, is another great place to get started. Then there's a more informal resource repository, BLExIM (Business Librarians Exchanging Instructional Materials), that I helped to organize where business librarians can share instruction resources they've already created with one another. Finally, I would recommend that librarians look within their own organization for tools, departments, and people to help them with building learning objects for business information literacy. It's helpful to identify potential stakeholders and collaborators if you want to create something with staying power.

Question 5: What advice do you have for academic libraries supporting students interested in business research especially in entrepreneurship and small businesses?
Kara: If academic libraries are serious about supporting students in entrepreneurship and small business, then I would suggest having a dedicated subject specialist on staff. Business reference is niche, and there are so many resources out there. It's worth it to have someone who can help students navigate them. At my institution, I'm the only business librarian, and I know that many of my colleagues are in the same situation. Depending on the scale of the programs, it would be ideal to have more than one person specializing in these areas. I just don't think it's realistic or sustainable to expect successful programs in entrepreneurship or small business if you don't have knowledge specialists in these areas to support the students.

Question 6: Anything else we did not get to talk about that you want to share?
Kara: Connecting what students learn in the classroom to actual skills they will need in the workforce is so important. I think the toolkit helps to do that in the way it's formatted, and the content in the elective modules is especially created for that purpose. If anyone out there reading this is interested, the complete canvas course file for the Business Research Toolkit is available to download from BLExIM, and I'm always happy to discuss ideas and share whatever I can with others interested in building business information literacy programs.

An Interview with Monika Chavez, Career Education Librarian, Mt. San Antonio College, California

Question 1: Thank you for speaking with us! Can you tell us about your role? How do you support career-seeking community members in your library at Mt. San Antonio College? Are there workshops that you provide?
Monika: I am the Career Education Librarian at Mt. San Antonio College, a large community college in eastern Los Angeles County, California. Essentially my role at the Library centers on the needs of Career Education programs at the college. These include nursing and allied health, aeronautics, agriculture, culinary arts, and other programs that tie directly to specific careers. While I am not the liaison for every Career Education program, I coordinate projects that focus on Career Education such as the Library's Perkins and Strong Workforce grants, and I serve on related campus wide committees. Currently, my

main goal is to reach programs that have not traditionally incorporated the Library into their instruction. This includes creating research guides, customizing and teaching a library instruction session, or just popping into say hello for a few minutes.

We mainly support career-seeking community members in exploring careers, connecting them to campus resources (e.g., Admissions, Career Center, Continuing Education), and finding resources to study for career-related tests and credentials. While we do not have standalone workshops on careers, we teach instruction sessions for classes with career research assignments.

Question 2: What is a tool (or tools) that you commonly refer to or use?
Monika: For career exploration, I direct students to Ferguson's Career Guidance Center. This database includes information on career exploration, education planning, and gaining skills for the job market such as writing resumes and networking. I particularly like their Profession Profiles. They are easy-to-read overviews of professions, including quick facts like minimum education level, certification or licensing, skills, and salary.

For career-related tests or credentials, I refer students to PrepSTEP for Community Colleges. It contains practice tests and study materials for a variety of career fields including nursing, respiratory therapy, radiologic technology, real estate, and veterinary technology.

Question 3: How do you engage with your learners on career research or education? What is often the most common issue that students experience when it comes to career research/education?
Monika: To engage with learners, I encourage curiosity and exploration. In my role, I am not requiring them to give me an answer; my goal is to guide them toward the resources that help them discover and reflect.

A common issue I see is students feeling overwhelmed when choosing a career. They do not want to make the "wrong" choice. In these cases, I let them know that finding a career is not always a straight shot, sometimes there are detours. At times, the best thing to do is to listen, and I aim to make students feel heard.

Question 4: Do you partner with Mr. San Antonio College Career Services? If so, can you tell us about your partnership with them?
Monika: While we do not currently partner with the Career Center, we maintain a good relationship with them. Though we answer career-related questions at the Library, we refer students and alumni to the Career Center when we believe they will be better served by their expertise and resources—especially when it comes to finding and applying for jobs.

Question 5: What advice do you have for academic libraries supporting students who are job seekers or career education/research?
Monika: My advice is to share your career journeys. Students can feel intimidated or overwhelmed when it comes to careers. People spend a significant portion of their lives at work! By sharing my journey, I hope to show students that I was once where they are. We all start somewhere. Of course, I do not just blurt out my experience. In instruction sessions, I will relate my own experiences when going through resources. For example, I will mention transferable skills, and how my retail experience helped equip me with skills to work with people at the Library. In one-on-one sessions, if I have a rapport with a student, I will mention my own experience. I think it also makes students feel more comfortable asking questions.

Question 6: Is there anything else that you would like to talk about that we did not get to discuss?
Monika: I would like to spotlight continuing education/noncredit. At Mt. San Antonio College, students can take tuition-free classes that lead directly to careers. Programs include training/certification to become emergency medical technicians, pharmacy technicians, solar panel technicians, and floral designers. While continuing education/noncredit is not always tuition-free, I highly recommend exploring the resources available in your area.

An Interview with Rebecca Hastie, Information Literacy Librarian, American University of Sharjah, United Arab Emirates

Question 1: Thank you for speaking with us! Can you tell us about your role at the American University of Sharjah?
Rebecca: As the Information Literacy Librarian at the American University of Sharjah, I have a multifaceted role in promoting information literacy. This includes overseeing the Information Literacy (IL) workshop program integrated into the General Education curriculum. These workshops, delivered across three core writing courses, are designed to develop students' understanding of the online information landscape and hone their library database skills in their first year, advancing to more complex search techniques and information evaluation skills in their second year. The high workload of teaching these workshops (reaching as many as 60 per semester) is managed by myself, my teaching assistant, and another full-time librarian. It's crucial that the content not only resonates with all students across the courses but is also consistently deliverable by any one of us. I'm also dedicated to continually updating the workshop content and exercises, ensuring they remain relevant and effective.

I also lead various workshop programs tailored for students, staff, and faculty, with a focus on information literacy. These workshops cover topics like AI, effective Wikipedia usage, optimizing Google search techniques, and identifying misinformation and disinformation.

My role extends into organizing various student-focused events. This includes orientation programs, first-year experience initiatives, and fun activities to help alleviate student stress during exam periods. One of my favorite parts of my role has been creating and running an escape room experience for orientation, which creatively engages new students with the library's resources and services.

I've really enjoyed the unique experiences that come with this role, like the time I was a judge in a cosplay contest! It's always a pleasure to connect with AUS' diverse community and highlight the crucial role of information literacy in different settings.

Question 2: With AI, I know you offered workshops for students to explore AI for Job Hunting. Can you tell us about this workshop?
Rebecca: The workshop, *Using AI to Job Hunt,* was the fourth and final session of my *"AI Amplified"* series. The goal of the workshop was to empower students with the skills needed to navigate today's (and tomorrow's) job market effectively by educating students about how employers are using AI tools in their recruitment processes and how students can use AI with their applications and interview preparations as they prepare to enter the workforce. *"Using AI to Job Hunt"* focused on four key areas:

1. ***AI screening in job applications:*** I explained how many employers are increasingly using AI to screen job applicants. This involves using AI to analyze resumes and cover letters, not just for keywords relating to the job, but also to assess suggested personality traits. I emphasized the importance of having cover letters and resumes that are well-structured and optimized with the right keywords to meet the requirements of any screening systems that may be in use.
2. ***Discovering jobs with AI platforms:*** I introduced AI tools that use algorithms to scan a user's application materials and suggest job listings based on identified skills and user preferences.
3. ***Creating and evaluating application materials with AI:*** Participants practiced using AI tools to create cover letters and resumes. They were provided with a fictional job applicant and a mock cover letter and resume as examples. Participants learned to input job experience into AI platforms to generate application templates populated with their applicant details and edit them to ensure they are accurate and personable. They then used AI tools to evaluate their documents with the job listing, ensuring they met the desired criteria of the job requirements and included the right keywords to make it past potential AI screening systems.

4. ***Using AI in interview preparation:*** I shared prompts that can be used in generative AI chatbots to conduct mock interviews. This included asking AI to role-play as a prospective employer by asking common interview questions and providing feedback on answers given. Participants also practiced using AI to help craft anecdotes into interview-friendly responses using the STAR method.

Question 3: You also offer skill based training workshops like creating presentations using AI. How do you see libraries' role in including AI tools? Was it a challenge to learn how to use them for yourself?
Rebecca: As a librarians' role is to guide information discovery, use and creation effectively, I believe it is vital for us to stay up-to-date with technological advancements, including AI, and to integrate AI tools into our practice and instruction. I find that most AI tools are designed with user-friendly intuitive interfaces, meaning that myself and workshop participants are able to quickly navigate different platforms without instruction. There are, of course, other challenges.

One prominent challenge is determining which tools are worth investing in, both in terms of time and financial resources. The AI field is rapidly evolving, with new tools constantly emerging. It can be difficult to discern which platforms are genuinely useful with longevity versus those quickly developed for profit. Another challenge is the financial aspect. Many AI tools are behind paywalls, which can limit access for both librarians and users.

To navigate this I have focused on emphasizing learning and teaching general AI skills, such as effective prompt engineering, rather than focusing on the specifics of any single platform. For example, in my workshop on creating presentations with AI, I identified common features across various generative AI presentation and image creation tools and aimed to teach prompts that work in all of my chosen software examples rather than precise how-to instructions for each tool. I also choose to use platforms that offer free access, or at least have a generous free trial period, for hands-on activities to keep them accessible to students. I try not to use platforms that require users to create memberships but these are unfortunately very rare.

Navigating the fast-moving and unpredictable AI landscape can certainly be daunting, not least due to the significant time commitment required for continuous skill development. I am fortunate that my workplace has been supportive of my self-directed AI education, and I am eager to complement this with formal professional training. I think the best way we can overcome the challenges posed by AI is by fostering a collaborative environment to collectively share our new knowledge, teaching successes, and growing expertise in AI, supporting our holistic development as a profession in this area.

Question 4: What advice do you have for academic libraries supporting students who are job seekers or career education/research? What should we think about generative AI tools?
Rebecca: As academic librarians our goals align with the wider university in supporting student's career readiness and preparation. I believe that the ability to navigate rapidly changing information environments, including effective use of AI tools, has become an essential employability skill. These generative AI tools, when used properly, serve as valuable assets for boosting efficiency and streamlining administrative tasks, ultimately leaving more room for human skills such as critical thinking, analysis, problem-solving, and innovation.

Academic libraries play a pivotal role as facilitators in nurturing adaptable, information-literate individuals who can adeptly utilize and harness the power of AI tools. This approach ensures that students not only possess the skills to use AI but also comprehend its broader impact within their respective fields and understand how to use these tools productively and responsibly.

While we have always supported the development of skills such as critical thinking, creativity, and adaptability through our information literacy instruction, it is now important that we directly link our library support to AI and careers. This connection allows us to demonstrate the tangible value of our instruction, highlighting our pivotal role in preparing students for the dynamic demands of the modern workforce.

Question 5: Anything else you like to talk about that we did not get to discuss?
Rebecca: There's a critical aspect of AI's impact that cannot be understated: the acceleration of misinformation and disinformation. Generative AI tools have the potential to spread false information at an unprecedented pace. The consequences of this rapid dissemination of misleading content can be far-reaching and, in some cases, devastating. As information professionals our role in combating this issue is more crucial than ever.

I believe that information literacy is a key defense against the spread of misinformation and disinformation. It's essential that we empower our communities, which undoubtedly include tomorrow's leaders, with the skills to seek, evaluate, and create information that will counter harmful misinformation and disinformation.

In facing the critical issue of misinformation and disinformation accelerated by AI, it's important not to feel overwhelmed. While the online information landscape evolves rapidly, our approach remains consistent. We must continue reinforcing and teaching the same core principles of information literacy—critical thinking, source evaluation, and an understanding of information creation and dissemination. These skills, already in our toolkit, are our strongest defense against the challenges posed by generative AI. Our profession has always adapted to change, and this is no different. We have the means to address AI-related issues through the application of existing information literacy skills. It's a matter of adapting our expertise to this evolving information environment.

CHAPTER SUMMARY

In this chapter, we review specific topics in career information literacy, where you can apply your instructional practices to engage with your learners. This may include specific lessons and training and case studies to consider for your career services regardless of library type. We specifically call attention to the need for programs and services beyond the resume and cover letter support to actively partner and support learners through career centers or within your public libraries for wider community interest and engagement.

NOTES

1. Forster, Marc, ed. *Information Literacy in the Workplace*. United Kingdom: Facet Publishing, 2017, 29.
2. Ibid., 141.
3. "AI Leadership Brief." *Urban Libraries Council*, October 2023. Accessed at https://www.urbanlibraries.org/files/AI_Leadership-Brief_October2023.pdf.
4. Queens Public Library. "Incorporating ChatGPT in the Workplace." *Twitter Post*, August 23, 2023. Accessed at https://twitter.com/QPLNYC/status/1690460485936664578.
5. Carter, Alex. "Microsoft Representatives Hold AI Workshop at Topeka & Shawnee County Public Library." *WIBW*, November 2, 2023. Accessed at https://www.wibw.com/2023/11/02/microsoft-representatives-hold-ai-workshop-topeka-shawnee-county-public-library/?fbclid=IwAR3KKfJp-DMyxB4wr7_krUwn6h9Gzfd1C96cdi-kreUC7CLYA8nTVPPIQAE_aem_AWPFM5zLnij_1AvxbrZuNKXoiqSUAmpX9tb87QROTz6omTrS1MkWh091szzclEOq2JE.
6. Ohio State University. "Major Decisions: Facts & Figures about Students Changing Majors." Accessed at https://exploration.osu.edu/Breaking%20Up%20Is%20Hard%20to%20Do/Changing%20Majors%201.14.pdf.
7. Alvarez, Barbara A. *Embedded Business Librarianship for the Public Librarian*. Chicago, IL: ALA Editions, 2016, 6.
8. Narlock, Mikala, and Mark Robison. "Liaison Librarianship in Shiny Packages: An Exploration of Product Ownership in Academic Libraries." *International Information & Library Review*, vol. 54, no. 1 (2022): 83.
9. Cox, Fannie M. "Unrecognized Roles of Libraries in Collaboration to Improve." In *Library Collaborations and Community Partnerships: Enhancing Health and Quality of Life*, edited by Vicki Hines-Martin, Fannie M. Cox, and Henry R. Cunningham, 10. New York, NY: Routledge, 2020.
10. Cox, Fannie M. "Unrecognized Roles of Libraries in Collaboration to Improve." Page 7.
11. Pun, Raymond, See Xiong, Adan Ortega, and Vanna Nauk. "Doing Technology: A Teaching Collaboration between Fresno State and Fresno County Public Library."

College & Research Libraries News, vol. 78, no. 6 (June 6, 2017). Accessed at https://crln.acrl.org/index.php/crlnews/article/view/16677.
12. "California Wraparound." California Department of Social Services. Accessed at https://www.cdss.ca.gov/inforesources/cdss-programs/foster-care/wraparound.
13. Public Library Association. "Partnering to Meet Community Workforce Needs." October 5, 2023. Accessed at https://www.ala.org/pla/education/onlinelearning/webinars/ondemand/partnering.
14. Pun, Raymond. "Mapping Collaborations Between Academic Business Libraries and Career Centres: An Exploratory Study." 2017, 8. Accessed at https://library.ifla.org/id/eprint/2769/1/s05-2019-pun-en.pdf.
15. Partners for Rural Impact. "2024 Rural Summit: From Cradle to Career." Accessed at https://web.cvent.com/event/caec6588-98be-41fc-a1b4-d8ca65824869/websitePage:3d6d2182-5322-49db-bc62-7309541129c3.
16. Partners for Rural Impact. "APPC2C Appalachian Cradle-to-Career Partnership." Accessed at https://partnersrural.org/appc2c/.
17. University of Wyoming Libraries. "Wyoming Library of Business." October 14, 2021. Accessed at https://www.uwyo.edu/libraries/about/news-events/2021/10/wyoming-library-to-business.html.
18. U.S. Census Bureau. "Veterans News." September 17, 2023. Accessed at https://www.census.gov/topics/population/veterans/news-updates/news.html
19. LeMire, Sarah, and Kristen J. Mulvihill. *Serving Those Who Served: Librarian's Guide to Working with Veteran and Military Communities.* New York, NY: Libraries Unlimited, 2017, 70.
20. National Alliance to End Homelessness. "State of Homelessness: 2023 Edition." September 17, 2023. Accessed at https://endhomelessness.org/homelessness-in-america/homelessness-statistics/state-of-homelessness/.
21. Orange County Housing Authority. "2023 Waiting List Opening." October 5, 2023. Accessed at https://www.ochousing.org/2023-waiting-list-opening.
22. Suzuki, Emi, and Caroline Sergeant. "New UNHCR Data Points to Record Number of Worldwide Refugees in 2022 Driven Largely by the War in Ukraine." *World Bank Blogs*, June 20, 2023. Accessed at https://blogs.worldbank.org/opendata/new-data-unhcr-points-record-high-number-worldwide-refugees-2022#:~:text=According%20to%20the%20newly%20released,from%2027.1%20million%20in%202021.
23. Executive Office for Immigration Review, US Department of Justice. "Recognized Organizations and Accredited Representatives Roster by State and City." Accessed at https://www.justice.gov/eoir/recognized-organizations-and-accredited-representatives-roster-state-and-city.
    immi. Free and simple information for immigrants. "About Immi." Accessed at https://www.immi.org/en/Info/About.
24. Madison Public Library. "Centro Hispano—Immigration Services." Accessed at https://www.madisonpubliclibrary.org/resources/eresources/centro-hispano-immigration-services#:~:text=Centro%20Hispano%20offers%20immigration%20services,service%20has%20a%20minimum%20cost.
25. Ghailan, Fatma. "Tools for the Job: The Role of Libraries in Upskilling Adults." *American Libraries*, May 2021, 49.
26. Ibid.

27. Devon County Council. "New Libraries Work Club Launch for Refugee Week." Accessed June 20, 2023, at https://www.devon.gov.uk/news/new-libraries-work-club-launch-for-refugee-week/.
28. Government of Canada. "Library Settlement Partnerships." Accessed September 17, 2023. https://www.canada.ca/en/immigration-refugees-citizenship/corporate/partners-service-providers/immigrant-serving-organizations/best-practices/library-settlement-partnerships.html.
29. Couloute, Lucius, and Daniel Kopf. "Out of Prison & Out of Work: Unemployment among Formerly Incarcerated People." Accessed October 5, 2023. https://www.prisonpolicy.org/reports/outofwork.html#:~:text=Using%20a%20nationally%20representative%20dataset,living%20in%20the%20United%20States.
30. Dholakia, Nazish. "New Partnerships Help Incarcerated People Find Jobs." Accessed October 5, 2023. https://www.vera.org/news/new-partnerships-help-incarcerated-people-find-jobs?fbclid=IwAR11DUyDiMoJ0SgmCzwh8--XuRwb2IDha5gz-rgMv-xl_XhGA6yCLVZnkAUc.
31. Institute for Justice. "From Barred Working: A Nationwide Study of Occupational Licensing Barriers for Ex-Offenders." Accessed October 5, 2023. https://ij.org/report/barred-from-working/.
32. Austin, Jeanie. *Library Services and Incarceration: Recognizing Barriers, Strengthening Access.* Chicago, IL: ALA Neal-Schuman, 2021, 140.
    Lilienthal. "Prison and Public Libraries." 2013. Accessed at https://www.libraryjournal.com/story/prison-and-public-libraries.
33. Lim, Taffany, and Raymond Pun. "An Interview with Taffany Lim, Executive Director for Cal State LA Center for Engagement." September 15, 2021. Accessed at https://sllibrarian.uni.edu/articles/202109/interview-taffany-lim-executive-director-cal-state-la-center-engagement.
34. Dixon, Duffy. "A New Start: Formerly Incarcerated Individuals Find Opportunities with Entrepreneurship Director." *American Libraries*, November 1, 2023. Accessed at https://americanlibrariesmagazine.org/2023/11/01/a-new-start/.
35. Leppert, Rebecca, and Katherine Schaeffer. "Pew Research Center. 8 Facts about Americans with Disabilities." July 24, 2023. Accessed at https://pewrsr.ch/3Qg5vLX
36. Northwestern Polytechnic. "Non-essential vs. Essential Duties." Adapted from the Learning Portal created by College Libraries Ontario. Content has been adapted for the NWP Learning Commons in June 2021. Accessed at https://libguides.nwpolytech.ca/career/essentialduties.
37. Adler, Mike. "Toronto Public Library's First Job Expo for People on Autism Spectrum Provides Welcoming Space 'to Be Yourself'." *Toronto.com,* October 23, 2023. Updated October 23, 2023. Accessed at https://www.toronto.com/things-to-do/toronto-public-librarys-first-job-expo-for-people-on-autism-spectrum-provides-welcoming-space-to/article_f6486fc7-09e2-5b68-a009-176abd7f353d.html?
38. LifeWorks. "DO MORE Than You Ever Thought Possible." Accessed at https://www.lifeworks.org/.
39. MIT Technology Licensing Office. "2023 IAP Intellectual Property Speaker Series." October 5, 2023. Accessed at https://tlo.mit.edu/iap2023?utm_source=website&utm_medium=linkedin&utm_campaign=iap2023.

40. Gale. "Gale Small Business Resources." October 5, 2023. Accessed at https://www.gale.com/databases/gale-business.
41. BRASS Business Guide. "Small Business & Entrepreneurship." Accessed at https://brass.libguides.com/SmallBusinessCore.
42. New York Public Library. "NYC Small Business Resource Center." Accessed at https://www.nypl.org/help/services/smallbiz.
43. Enoch Pratt Free Library. "Entrepreneur Academy." October 5, 2023. Accessed at https://www.prattlibrary.org/entrepreneur-academy.
44. Queens Chamber of Commerce. "Hollis Business Resources Day: Multilingual Materials for Small Business in Queens." Accessed at https://www.nyc.gov/assets/dca/downloads/pdf/about/EventFlyer-HollisBusinessResourcesDay-033023.pdf.
45. Rivlin, Gary. *Saving Main Street: Small Business in the Time of COVID-19*. New York, NY: Harper Business, 2022, 321.
46. Rivlin, Gary, and Jessica Looze. "Are We Back? Early-Stage Entrepreneurship Trends Two Years into the COVID Pandemic." 2022. Accessed at https://www.kauffman.org/entrepreneurship/reports/are-we-back-entrepreneurship-trends-covid-pandemic.
47. Sull, Donald, Charles Sull, and Ben Zweig. "Toxic Culture Is Driving the Great Resignation." *MIT Sloan Management Review*, 2022. Accessed at https://sloanreview.mit.edu/article/toxic-culture-is-driving-the-great-resignation/.

3

Workforce Development and Impact on Libraries

This chapter covers the following:

- Workforce development policies and programs nationally (in the United States) and globally
- Future workforce opportunities and skills for planning
- Advocacy work to support workforce development programs

When we think about new jobs coming in, the Department of Labor projected 2016-2026 with these new jobs coming in different sectors and industries. Centering how the library can support these job opportunities and advocate for economic development and workforce programs can yield great attention from stakeholders who determine funding allocations and citizen engagement. When libraries make differences in economic matters, it will garner attention and spotlight. However, advocacy work does not happen in a vacuum. It takes a lot of time and work to make it happen. We will explore how to leverage existing resources and policies to center library's influence and program in workforce development.

FUTURE OF WORKFORCE TRENDS: PLANNING AND SKILLS DEVELOPMENT FOR EMERGING INDUSTRIES

What do we know about future jobs? In chapter 2, there is a lesson plan focusing on future jobs and trends (see lesson 1.4c). We know there are external forces such as generative AI tools (like ChatGPT) that will shape future trends and opportunities. This part of the section helps you think about labor issues, trends, and opportunities to consider.

Visual Capitalist, a graphic design company, collected and analyzed data from the U.S. Chamber of Commerce from July 2023, and created a map called "The Best and Worst U.S. States for Job Seekers" in the United States to indicate which "states that are the best for job seekers, and each state's rate of available workers for every 100 job openings."[1]

The top five states listed North Dakota, South Dakota, Nebraska, Maryland, and New Hampshire. The bottom five states listed California, New York, New Jersey, Connecticut, and Washington. These bottom states may have more population densities and cities. As of August 2023, "there are 9.8 million open jobs in the U.S. and only 5.8 million unemployed workers."[2] Perhaps job seekers are willing to relocate to another state, and you may be able to connect and refer them to workforce programs in other states with greater opportunities than existing local areas. Although it is hard to predict how these trends may shift over time, this data gives you an estimate or consideration to mention how there are more workers in certain states than jobs currently available.

The factors of globalization, automation, and emerging technologies continue to reshape and disrupt the current workplace, workforce, and work itself. It requires conversations with stakeholders of experts, practitioners, policymakers, and industry leaders.

There are skill trends which are often important factors to consider. Many tend to be soft skill trends such as interpersonal skills, critical thinking, problem-solving, creativity, collaboration, emotional intelligence, and culturally competent skills. The Lego Foundation's Mirjam Schöning and Christina Witcomb wrote in the World Economic Forum that "play" is an important skill based on a study in New Zealand, which "compared children who learned how to read at age five with those who learned at age seven." Play encourages opportunities to develop these soft skills such as social, emotional, physical, and creative skills that can scaffold the complex soft skills. Creating playful moments and experiences in education can tremendously improve skill development and job prospects.

According to the *Future of Jobs Report* produced by the World Economic Forum, here were Top 10 Skills in 2020:

- Complex Problem-Solving
- Critical Thinking
- Creativity
- People Management
- Coordinating with Others
- Emotional Intelligence
- Judgment and Decision-Making
- Service Orientation
- Negotiation
- Cognitive Flexibility[3]

Times have changed from 2020 going forward but many expectations have changed and stayed similar too. *The Future of Jobs Report for 2023* found that there will be a lot of growth, disruption, and reskilling of workers, especially impacted by the environment and by technology. The following skills were listed as core skills in the workforce in this report:

1. Analytical thinking
2. Creative thinking
3. Resilience, flexibility, and agility
4. Motivation and self-awareness
5. Curiosity and lifelong learning
6. Technological literacy
7. Dependability and attention to detail
8. Empathy and active listening
9. Leadership and social influence
10. Quality control[4]

These job skills have transitioned again into other important industry demands. Business and Technology Advisor and Author Bernard Marr wrote in *Forbes Magazine* that in 2030, these are the important skills needed based on numerous sources:

- Digital Literacy
- Augmented Work
- Sustainable Work
- Critical Thinking and Analysis
- Data Skills
- Creative Thinking
- Emotional Intelligence
- Lifelong Learning
- Leadership Skills[5]

Soft skills continue to play an important role regardless if it is 2020 or 2030 and in developing one's career prospects. These skills are needed and can be developed and taught over time in library workshops or promoted from library and external resources (e.g., Coursera) to teach such skills if that is one way to engage with the community. How does this connect to job growth and outlook? According to the *U.S. Bureau of Labor's Occupational Outlook Handbook*, "Fastest growing occupations: 20 occupations with the highest projected percent change of employment between 2022-32," these are the positions and their growth rates that will be trending:

- Wind turbine service technicians at 45%
- Nurse practitioners at 45%

- Data scientists at 35%
- Statisticians at 32%
- Information security analysts at 32%
- Medical and health services manager at 27%
- Epidemiologists at 27%
- Physician assistant at 27%
- Software developers at 26%
- Occupational therapy assistant at 24%
- Actuaries at 22%
- Computer and information research scientists at 23%
- Operations research analysts at 23%
- Solar photovoltaic installers at 22%
- Home health and personal care aids at 22%
- Taxi drivers at 21%
- Personal care and service workers, all other at 21%
- Veterinary technologists and technicians at 21%
- Veterinary assistants and laboratory animal caretakers at 20%[6]

With this forecast, it may help you to consider partnering with industry leaders, practitioners, and trade groups/associations to promote these opportunities and skill development in the library and host relevant workshops focusing on these careers such as Q&A with the industry or skill building workshops. When you think about your work as a library advocate for a workforce development program, utilize this information and explain to stakeholders on how library resources and services can better support future job opportunities in the community.

Within the United States, If you are interested in skills development policy changes and support, consider exploring National Skills Coalition, an organization that

> organizes broad-based coalitions seeking to raise the skills of America's workers across a range of industries. We advocate for public policies that invest in what works, as informed by our members' real-world expertise. And we communicate these goals to an American public seeking a vision for a strong U.S. economy that allows everyone to be part of its success.[7]

The organization offers resources, networks, policy reports, events, webinars, and an action center to help you and your community promote workforce development programs in the legislative channel. You can sign up for their free newsletter to get information regarding the future of work, workforce data, immigration and skills, upskilling, and more.

Globally, there is an emphasis on the United Nations' (UN) Sustainable Development Goals (SDGs). The SDGs were adopted by the UN Member

States during the General Assembly of September 2015. There are seventeen goals and each goal represents critical areas that countries should accomplish by 2030. These goals include zero hunger, affordable and clean energy, quality education, and decent work and economic growth. From a big picture, we can see how libraries may want to align with the SDGs and support their communities in the process. The American Library Association's UN 2030 Sustainable Development Goals Task Force described how they serve as a community catalyst to "promote how libraries are uniquely positioned to raise awareness of the SDGs with their broad reach into communities."[8] Furthermore, libraries supporting workforce development are critical advocacy components. Under goal 8, decent work and economic growth and unemployment cases are rising globally. Libraries can play a role in providing skill training, job referrals, and support services.[9] When we think about global advocacy work, this goal can offer a touch point on how career services and workforce development programs in your library will meet a global goal.

Global Entrepreneurship Week (GNW), a global annual event that celebrates entrepreneurs and entrepreneurship in mid-November, can be a collaborative program to highlight the library's role supporting small business owners, entrepreneurs from the community, as well as entrepreneurship programs in a university. GNW can be planned ahead and used as an advocacy talking point to engage with your community members. You may want to host workshops, hold spaces for small business owners together, or offer spaces for them to showcase or sell their products if your library has space offered. These activities may require communication with different partners and coordinating schedules but it could be a way to highlight to your state assembly or city representatives on what your library is doing to promote workforce programs and supporting small businesses. In addition, nationally, November is known as National Entrepreneurship Month in the United States, where it is a time to celebrate and recognize entrepreneurs supporting their communities and that enriches the American economy. The library programs and events advocating for entrepreneurs can align with these celebrations and can be a day, a week, or a month long.

Another global factor impacting workforce programming is generative AI. We touched upon this topic briefly in chapter 1 and in chapter 2 (see lesson 1.4D). How will generative AI impact the workforce? In *Harvard Business Review*, New York University professor and author Amy Webb, writes, "How to Prepare for a GenAI Future You Can't Predict," and shares that "workforce change is an inevitable side effect of technological evolution, and leaders need a systemized way of seeing what the future of their organizations will look like in the wake of generative AI's developments."[10] There is an increasing approach to upskilling and identifying how we can leverage technology like generative AI to do basic prompts and functions that can be improved and become efficient as the technology improves too. In addition, there are tools that could be used during the job search process. Here are ones we found:

- Teal [https://www.tealhq.com/]—A resume builder and job application tracker that can be used by those who are applying for multiple jobs and personalizing their application.
- Prepper [https://www.adzuna.com/prepper]—Need to speak to someone to prepare for an interview? An interview coaching tool that can connect you with a chatbot who can serve as support.
- CoverLetter CoPilot [https://coverlettercopilot.ai/]—Similar to ChatGPT, CoverLetter CoPilot utilizes large language models (LLMs) like ChatGPT and serves as a writing assist especially useful for those writing cover letters, statements, or resumes.
- Rezi [https://www.rezi.ai/ai-resignation-letter-builder]—Thinking of resigning? Rezi is a resignation letter generator that can create a letter when you decide to leave your job.

There are other tools that will impact how we do work in the future because of generative AI tools as documented by *Forbes Magazine*.[11] We anticipate a growing number of tools and refinement of such responses over time. It is important to note that we do not know how the changes will affect our behaviors and work flows but it is important to be aware of them.

In August 2023, the Pew Research Center released survey results on Americans' perspectives on emerging technologies and uses of AI in jobs. The online survey was conducted among over 5,000 U.S. adults from July 17 to 23, 2023. One notable finding is that

> In the Center's new survey, about half or more of those who have heard of ChatGPT say chatbots will have a major impact on software engineers (56%), graphic designers (54%) and journalists (52%) over the next 20 years. Smaller shares think chatbots will have a major effect on teachers (44%) or lawyers (31%).[12]

With these jobs being potentially impacted by ChatGPT or other generative AI tools, it comes to mind how workforce development programs need to think of ways to prepare future employees on utilizing this tool effectively.

Another important finding in the report is that

> Americans are less likely to think chatbots will impact their own job. Some 19% of employed adults who have heard of ChatGPT think chatbots will have a major impact on their job. Another 36% say it will have a minor impact and 27% expect no impact at all.[13]

As of 2024, it is difficult to see how generative AI tools will impact the workforce completely since the technology is evolving with new versions coming out and advanced versions based on subscription models. What we do know is that generative AI tools will be used in some ways in the workplace, and libraries need to prepare job seekers in using these tools and advocate with stakeholders on the implications of such tools to ensure safeguarding an individual's privacy and their usage (ethical usage of these tools, surveillance concerns, labor exploitations, environmental and social implications, privacy data collections, etc.).

LIBRARY ADVOCACY WORK ON WORKFORCE DEVELOPMENT

What should library workers and community members do to advocate for workforce development internally and externally? Now that you have some of the issues you are aware of, let us talk about how to stay informed, and the strategies and examples of outreach to advocate and promote workforce development programs in your libraries.

To stay up-to-date with legislative issues regarding workforce developments such as the INVEST in American Act, Digital Equity Act, and so forth that are happening within the U.S. Congress, consider signing up for email alerts from the American Library Association Public Policy and Advocacy Office [https://www.ala.org/aboutala/offices/ppa] to write to your local stakeholders to support acts that help job creations and support.

EveryLibrary Institute [https://www.everylibraryinstitute.org/], a 501c3 organization that supports library funding in the United States, also has done a lot of advocacy work to support bills that positively impact libraries. You can sign up for their news alerts and updates too. In addition, check your state and regional chapters [https://www.ala.org/aboutala/affiliates/chapters/state/stateregional] and their legislative committees for updates to stay informed on what is happening locally in your area. There will be increasing bills and discussions such as AI, broadband, and infrastructure that will impact workforce development and libraries to come.

For strategic engagements, in September 2023, ALA released an advocacy action plan workbook for free for anyone to download and adapt as their own plan to advocate for awareness and ultimately for library funding to support workforce development programs.

> *The Advocacy Action Plan Workbook* is intended to help advocates plan effectively towards realization of specific goals. It is a project of ALA's Committee on Library Advocacy (COLA) and updates the 2009 *Advocacy Action Workbook*, developed by the American Library Association and United for Libraries.[14]
>
> Using a step-by-step approach, this free workbook is designed to help you think about setting goals, delivering the message, advocacy work, and conducting a community analysis.

When advocating for a workforce development program, consider external factors that may create barriers to job seekers such as lack of housing or child/elder care, experiencing food insecurity, language barriers, poverty, mental illness, or broadband exclusion, or having incarceration records. To support job seekers experiencing these issues, you have to think about these other issues that may prevent them from progressing into their work. How do you address these issues all at once? It feels overwhelming to think about these collective issues at once. It is important to recognize how these issues are interlocking and connected. One way to think about these issues is to advocate for issues locally via coalitions. All of these factors can be identified within the community and requires raising awareness and advocating for funding in addressing these areas. We recommend reading works such as *Before the Ballot: Building Political Support for Library Funding* (2019) by John Chrastka and Patrick "PC" Sweeney to develop more ideas on policy and political advocacy work for your library.

Another approach to use this *ALA Advocacy Action Workbook* is to start collecting data, information, and testimonials on the impact of your services. Quantitatively, you can keep track of how many users seek your services, at what length per session, and what their requests are and the results are if they share. This can be from the survey questionnaire you send before you meet with the user.

Qualitatively, if you have written testimonials of job seekers who have been able to obtain jobs or entrepreneurs who have started seeing their business take off because of library services and resources, these are the stories to collect and to share out in your reports, social media channels, or campaign for library funding.

Here is an example from Redwood City Public Library sharing a story in the Redwood City Library Foundation newsletter on how the library's makerspace supported an entrepreneur's career, "How the Makerspace Helped Launch a New Career." "Jason is thankful to Makerspace for inspiring him to start his new career. He said "It's very unusual for a library to have such amazing machinery available to patrons at no charge. It's a tremendous resource but it's the patrons, volunteers, and staff that really make it special.""[15] With the library user's consent, you can share these stories with different organizations to increase awareness and interest. Stakeholders like politicians will want to know more about your programs too, so consider compiling these testimonials and address how your library supports the community's economic health.

Building coalitions is key in establishing presence, awareness, and influence in your community. We will discuss and explore some groups to consider building rapport on the topic of job seekers and entrepreneurship. Patrick "PC" Sweeney and John Chrastka author of *Winning Elections & Influencing Politicians for Library Funding* (2017) recommend readers to make connections with a local Chamber of Commerce, a group of business networks made up of business owners who are concerned about the economic health of businesses and entrepreneurs in the community.

> The library and the ballot committee should spend time talking about the economic benefits of a library, the return on investment, services to entrepreneurs, the library as a business anchor and themes around economic freedom to this group to make the biggest impact.[16]

When you attend these meetings, it is an opportunity to seek out new library users and advocates and to inform what your library is doing today to engage on these topics for job seekers and building support for them and for entrepreneurs. Consider exploring the National Chamber of Commerce Directory [https://www.uschamber.com/co/chambers] to find local groups in the United States and reach out to find time to check in or to host the meeting in your library if you have space. For those outside of the United States, there may be a business agency or network in your community or an International Chambers of Commerce (ICC) where you can search for members there [https://iccwbo.org/].

On July 31, 2023, the White House released the "National Cyber Workforce and Education Strategy" to "address both immediate and long-term cyber workforce needs."[17] When identifying trends and issues in career development, government agencies may offer guidance, resources, and directions to consider. If you are identifying for an awareness of career development, consider forming activities and events on National Careers Week which runs in March, usually 6-11.

> National Careers Week is targeted at improving the level of careers education in schools and colleges, with evidence showing at government level that this is an area that needs improvement in order to ensure that future generations will benefit from quality, meaningful interactions that will help them to understand the links between courses, skills and the pathways they open up.[18]

For additional strategies, ALA offers ways to engage with different stakeholders. The new book *Libraries that Build Business: Advancing Small Business and Entrepreneurship in Public Libraries* (2022), published by ALA Editions in collaboration with ALA Public Policy and Advocacy Office, dives into library programs and services supporting business development, classes, and workshops to support entrepreneurship and small businesses. The book is a useful resource providing case studies from real examples of how libraries can set up these programs and services and advocate for more resources from the community. Though it is a public library focus, the book can offer useful examples for academic libraries to think about and see what community programs are available for business and entrepreneurship students.

In addition to ALA and PLA, The Urban Libraries Council (ULC) is another organization to explore. ULC is a nonprofit that provides a forum for library leaders to share best practices and innovative ideas that inspire programs that support learning, a strong economy, and an active democracy. ULC programs are recognized for "creating new frameworks that invigorate public libraries and their communities."[19] The 2023 Innovations Winner profiles suggest ways to highlight your library's efforts in workforce development. There is a category for "Workforce and Economic Development" highlighting libraries and the past efforts in engaging with these programs. You can use these examples to demonstrate the potential impact of your own workforce program by modeling after these award winning services.[20]

In the ULC website, there is a section for Workforce and Economic Development covering step by step on public libraries promoting "equitable economic mobility and offering programming and services for all local workers, jobseekers, entrepreneurs and business owners."[21] From toolkits to service designs, "Closing the Entrepreneurship Gap: Tools for Libraries" can be a useful starting point in thinking about engaging with these groups but most importantly thinking of advocating for these groups as well as promoting the library's efforts. In 2018, ULC launched "Strengthening Libraries as Entrepreneurial Hubs," which provides case studies and white papers on entrepreneurship programs in libraries.[22] This report provides library profiles and their contributions to the local community. By exploring existing case studies, you can make an argument on how your services could align with these contributions.[23] Another useful resource is the Business Value Calculator. Launched in 2022, this tool provides public libraries a way to measure, assess, and evaluate its contributions to economic development. A new version of this calculator will come out in August 2024.

At times, you may get unexpected guests and requests with limited time to organize. Some of these high stake events could promote your library's interest in economic development. For example, on March 3, 2023, the vice president of the United State, Kamala Harris, visited the San Francisco Public Library's Chinatown branch to convene a round table discussion with Asian American and Pacific Islander small business owners and to promote workforce development.[24]

> The San Francisco Office of Small Business contacted the Library two days prior and requested to hold the meeting at the Chinatown Branch. The Library was asked not to promote the event in advance or spread the news about the Vice President's visit for security reasons.

This example could offer important ways to center your library as a central economic force in your community by holding such conversations. San Francisco City Librarian Michael Lambert shares that there were fifteen small business owners including San Francisco Mayor London Breed, San Francisco

Supervisor Aaron Peskin, California State Assemblymember Phil Ting, and Library Commission President Connie Wolf, Library Commission Vice-President, Pete Huang. "It will create opportunities to bend some ears when advocating for money for library infrastructure. The $5 billion Build America's Libraries Act was not included in the 2022 budget resolution and reconciliation instructions."[25] Convening together with stakeholders that centers on your library's space and commitment can prove to be very useful in building relationships with constituents across sectors.

When advocating with external partners, there is a goal to keep in mind: advocacy work internally. Advocating for staff buy-in and to understand the library's goals is important. Advocacy work cannot be done by one person but rather a community of advocates. Staff needs to be aware of the resources and information support. Carolyn Tipps, a librarian from Plano Public Library in Texas, shared in a virtual presentation in Entrepreneurship and Libraries conference, "Shifting Library Staff Perspectives on Supporting Entrepreneurship" that growth mindset takes time gradually to introduce staff on the mission of these new engagement support. "We are not providing expertise nor training but thinking about what we have and to support entrepreneurship."[26] Tipps also recommended exploring existing resources in the library and how to partner with community groups to support the needs of others and how business owners could use these resources such as creating flyers, social media marketing, and more. *Libraries Build Business* from ALA offers an assessment tool for you to work on when building advocacy internally and staff buy-in. There are some other questions to consider:

- What jargon or acronyms are you using? (Avoid them if possible.)
- Does your staff/colleagues feel supported and feel confident in presenting the content?
- What are the gaps in providing such services? What partners, resources, or training is needed?
- Are there library associations like State Library Chapters, State Library Agencies, PLA or ALA that offer guidance in advocacy work?

Overall, advocacy work happens internally and externally. Engaging with library staff in order to better support this work and connect with stakeholders outside of the library ensures that the library can provide workforce development programs. This approach applies to library workers regardless of library types to advocate for workforce development.

HIGHER EDUCATION ADVOCACY WORK

Advocacy work within higher education is different from public library work and may be focused from within the library and with campus stakeholders.

How do you partner with faculty and career services to ensure that communications are afloat and that students and their career interests and research are centered into the services and projects in the library? There are multiple ways to do this:

- Partnering with program office and faculty to ensure work-based learning is supported.
- Partnering with the career services center is key and to advocate for more resources into such partnerships require patience and communications.

For partnering with program office, for example, when you see updates on campus about collaborative efforts such as, "[City University of New York] CUNY Launches $16 Million Public-Private Partnership to Improve Student Career Success and Bolster Economic Growth" (published September 2022), the library should play an active role and connect with the stakeholders to engage with these initiatives to support the goals of this project. In the report, the CUNY chancellor stated,

> the Inclusive Economy Initiative builds on proven models for connecting students to in-demand careers and expanding the capacity of CUNY campuses to grow and sustain talent pipelines with employers across multiple fast-growing sectors—such as tech, healthcare and green jobs.[27]

The library can play a role in offering career research workshops or coordinating career research resources such as research guides and referral processes to students and faculty. For example, Frans Albarillo, a librarian at CUNY Brooklyn College, created a Job & Careers research guide that highlights Career One Stop, Federal Resources, Veteran Resources, and Student Jobs at the Library.[28] It is important to take on top of the campus news and updates by subscribing to the university's newsletters or student newspaper. By proactively engaging with external stakeholders interested in these initiatives for career success, libraries can partner and leverage its resources to support students' needs.

Emerging research and trends focusing on student engagement and success have included workplace-based learning, where faculty can incorporate assignments and projects centering on learning technical, academic, and employability skills in the classrooms for students to develop and apply in a real work environment. On October 10, 2023, ITHAKA S+R's Michael Field writes,

> The Council of Independent Colleges (CIC), with generous support from Strada Education Foundation and Ascendium Education Group, is piloting a newer form of experiential learning—virtual work-based

learning—with 25 small to midsize, independent colleges and universities. The Work-Based Learning Consortium provides participating institutions with access to Riipen, an online experiential learning marketplace and platform that matches instructors with organizations and employers to provide students with real-world learning opportunities.[29]

Libraries can support these efforts by introducing and teaching research skills relevant for specific classes and to encourage students to investigate career research. These new collaborations can be advocated by the library as well as departments and administrations involved to ensure that students' skills, career interests, and developments are centered across the academic programs.

In addition, high impact practices (HIPs) started as higher education trends and are now incorporated as critical practices in heightening student learning and academic development. HIPs are

> based on evidence of significant educational benefits for students who participate in them—including and especially those from demographic groups historically underserved by higher education. These [11] practices take many different forms, depending on learner characteristics and on institutional priorities and contexts.[30]

- Capstone Courses and Projects
- Collaborative Assignments and Projects
- Common Intellectual Experiences
- Diversity/Global Learning
- ePortfolios
- First-Year Seminars and Experiences
- Internships
- Learning Communities
- Service Learning, Community-Based Learning
- Undergraduate Research
- Writing-Intensive Courses

Most of these are geared toward the faculty, class, and academic programs. The relevant ones to become career development areas for advocacy with faculty and campus administrators include the internship and e-portfolio. For internships, libraries can partner with career development centers or services to offer workshops to teach students how to conduct industry or company research and to prepare for such internship opportunities when it comes to research skills.

In addition, libraries may help identify tools that can create e-portfolios (in partnership with the faculty and academic technology services or information technology groups) to develop a repository to showcase students' collection of works. If your institution already has an institutional repository such as Dspace or Digital Commons, consider the workflow of including class materials from students to highlight e-portfolios for specific classes. HIPs can be an effective advocacy talking point to alert faculty, career services, and other stakeholders on what the library can provide and support to ensure that students' career interests are met through library resources and services too. For a case study for a library in partnership with a faculty to support career development for a class, consider reading this article by academic librarian from Vanderbilt University HD McKay.[31] McKay writes "helping students prepare a strong portfolio of work to showcase their abilities could help them stand out in these fields."[32] This case study does not directly speak to HIPs, but it connects to this important role that libraries can play in supporting real work experiences and career development.

If you are seeking for a more specific level of engagement and advocacy, consider tapping into business librarians. Business librarians may consider exploring the Association to Advance Collegiate Schools of Business (AACSB International) and to examine their business school accreditation standards and how business librarians can play a role in supporting these efforts through information literacy instruction workshops and to foster critical and creative thinking and research.[33] By understanding more about AACSB to connect to the greater themes of lifelong learning and career development, business librarians can advocate for the library's role in supporting and collaborating with career services centers and business programs for accreditation purposes. BRASS is also another resource to explore for guidelines on teaching business information literacy and business information services. If your library does not have a dedicated business librarian, it is crucial to think and consider the potential of this position to collaborate with campus partners to foster entrepreneurship and career development.[34] Librarians can participate in the Entrepreneurship & Libraries Conference (held annually virtually) and develop ideas on engagement and advocacy strategies from a community of practice.[35] In the next chapter, we will review resources and training that might be helpful.

In addition, subject librarians outside of the business field can also partner with the career services centers and faculty to advocate for these high impact practices for specific careers. As we explored in the previous chapter, there are numerous ways to engage with different learners from various majors. Librarians who are in the health sciences field or liaison to vocational majors can consider collaborations as part of their work to support student success and retention. Although it takes time to build relationships, it does not mean it is limited to only business librarians.

Advocacy work within higher education is truly a collaborative process that takes place internally and externally. Internally, you need to partner with stakeholders and raise awareness and concern to engage with stakeholders externally (students, administrators, etc.), and for them to see how the library plays a tremendous value in supporting career development, higher education trends, and issues. At the end, it comes down to communications and collaborations.

INTERVIEWS AND PROFILES

In these next interviews, profiles, and case studies, we highlight how librarians from academic, government, and public libraries advocate for workforce development. We interviewed Lori Fisher, Megan Janicki, and Dr. Corinthia Price.

An Interview with Lori Fisher, State Librarian of Maine

At the state level, one example that connects among the state library, government agencies and local libraries is in Maine: "Maine State LIbrary and Department of Economic and Community Development Announce $1.7M in Maine Jobs & Recovery Plan Grants to Support Remote Work at Local Libraries."[36] In this interview, we speak with Lori Fisher, State Librarian of Maine, to talk about advocacy work for workforce development.

Question 1: Can you tell us about your role as a State Librarian? How do you support libraries' workforce development efforts?
Lori: State libraries take on a variety of different roles around workforce development. One of our primary roles is supporting libraries/library staff with efforts in their local communities through awareness of programs, projects, and services available. We also provide training around digital resources that support workforce development, and connect local libraries with county, state, regional, and national resources and funding opportunities. Maine State Library has had success in partnering with the Maine Department of Labor to provide training and awareness around statewide databases that regional career centers offer to Maine residents, and public libraries host Career Center staff for "office hours" where these staff have one-to-one coaching sessions with job seekers. My job as State Librarian is to identify opportunities to not only highlight what we already provide, but to promote the use of existing infrastructure in local communities (public libraries) to leverage the impact of new initiatives from other government agencies surrounding co-working, small business development, and entrepreneur support.

**Question 2: We are very pleased to see this happening in your state, "Maine Jobs & Recovery Plan Grants to Support Remote Work at Local Libraries" as published on August 3, 2023 in the Maine Department of Economic and Community Development. Can you share with us the role of the State Librarian and State Library in advocating for these programs and forming these

collaborations with the Maine Governor? What impact do you hope to see happen with these grants given to libraries located in rural, suburban, urban areas?

Lori: Advocating for our libraries is one of my most important roles as State Librarian. Quite often this takes the form of explaining what libraries "do" in terms that my colleagues in other agencies can relate to. I try to connect library work with their respective priorities so that they can begin to see libraries as another resource to help accomplish their goals. At the same time, it's equally important to make sure that libraries are provided with resources themselves so it's not just a case of, "here is this amazing infrastructure in virtually every corner of the state- feel free to leverage it" but more along the lines of, "libraries are ready partners and to make sure they have the capacity to support this initiative, we need to include additional resources for the libraries." With the Remote Work through Libraries initiative, we were able to work with the DECD team to ensure funds could be used for renovating existing space, new construction, staff time for the project, as well as things like furniture, new technology, and marketing. Here is an example of thinking creatively with this opportunity to benefit libraries and their communities long term beyond the focus on remote work. Many of our libraries struggle with basic facilities' needs- upgraded HVAC or electrical and ADA compliance, for example. Addressing these facilities issues are eligible expenses in this project. We had a library incorporate the addition of solar panels to offset the increased electrical costs of their space renovation. We've had several libraries purchase heat pumps. Not only do these purchases add to the space dedicated for remote workers (the primary focus of the initiative), they contribute to the long-term health of the library. We are also able to highlight how libraries are contributing to the goals of our Governor's Climate Action Plan.

Another impact is emphasizing how this program highlights the many ways libraries are addressing local, regional, and state priorities. We are working with the libraries to hone their own advocacy skills so they can use this experience to demonstrate their value to the economic vitality of their communities. The thirty-nine libraries participating in this initiative have designed their projects with the needs of their communities at the center. As such, we are hopeful that in the end we will have multiple models of how libraries can provide services for Maine's remote and hybrid workers. We were able to award grants to libraries in each of Maine's counties so we'll be able to show impact in all areas of the state. The governor's focus on making Maine a state that is attractive to remote workers (workers working from home for a Maine industry, operating a business from their home, and/or workers residing in Maine and working for an outside industry) necessarily needs to address areas of the state where there are fewer or no existing options for these workers. Libraries were a natural place to explore. The participating libraries are not only adding new space/renovating critical aspects of their buildings, they are making new partnerships and expanding their reach to previously unserved patrons.

Question 3: Can you tell us the importance of advocacy work in securing funding for these library projects especially related to workforce development? What are your strategies for speaking with stakeholders about the importance of libraries supporting small business owners, entrepreneurs and the economy?

Lori: My staff has emphasized the unique role public libraries play in local communities, especially in states like Maine where local control of local tax dollars is the norm. With 65% of our public libraries serving communities of under 5,000 residents, those libraries are usually the only source of free Internet, information, and technology help in small rural communities. Libraries are an integral part of the infrastructure needed to support any small business, entrepreneur, or co-working effort. Where else in a small rural community can you go to print something when your printer breaks? Or connect to the Internet when your home Internet service is not working? Libraries meet people where they are at, and that is critically important to highlight when looking at local solutions to improve workforce development as well as economic development. The key is to help people see how working with libraries furthers their own priorities. As an advocate we need to be able to help libraries demonstrate that, and at the same time, it is important to acknowledge what libraries may need to be successful partners. This is the "ask" in our advocacy work. While we know that libraries have been offering services that help small businesses for a long time, the focus now on the remote workforce, whether hybrid or fully remote, is raising new possibilities for driving economic development in our rural state. Additionally in Maine, almost 70% of our business economy depends on small businesses. We can help communities think creatively about how to support both of these types of workers.

Question 4: What are your thoughts on public and state library partnerships? You've previously served as a Director of a Public Library and now as a State Librarian, do you see this kind of partnership differently and have been able to leverage those experiences to speak with public librarians on important matters like workforce development?

Lori: There are definitely things that a state library can and cannot do, depending upon the organizational and funding structure in each state. For example, as an independent agency, Maine State Library has more opportunity to quickly partner with other entities. That was an asset in our discussions about the Maine Department of Economic and Community Development ARPA funds for the workforce development project. State libraries that exist within other larger entities such as a Department of Education or a Secretary of State's office have more bureaucracy to get through to obtain approval for partnerships or joint projects. But no matter what the mechanism is for partnership, I hope that public librarians understand that a state library always has to put the good of all libraries in the state at the forefront of our decision-making. This is how Maine has been able to make such great progress in programmatic areas such as Integrated Library System sharing, statewide van delivery, statewide online resource collections, and now workforce development.

Question 5: Anything else we didn't get to talk about that you want to share?
Lori: It is critical that libraries and library staff stop the siloed narrative that focuses exclusively on our services or what is in our buildings. What we do is about people. We need to illustrate both quantitatively and qualitatively the impact we can have on local areas of concern such as workforce development. To do that, relationship-building is key. Asking what community priorities exist, listening to the answers, and then thoughtfully identifying how the library can or is already contributing to the solution is very important. It's not enough to hope that a potential partner will come to a library and ask for help. Library leaders need to get out into their communities, listen to community members, and actively offer ways to be part of solutions to local/regional/state issues.

An Interview with Megan Janicki, Deputy Director, Strategic Initiatives at the American Library Association
Library associations play an important role in facilitating connections, resources, and collaborations. In this interview, Megan Janicki from the ALA will talk about how libraries are supporting workforce development.

Question 1: Thanks for speaking with us! Can you please tell us a bit about your role as Deputy Director, Strategic Initiatives at the American Library Association, Public Policy and Advocacy Office?
Megan: Thank you for this opportunity! I work at ALA's Public Policy and Advocacy office, located in Washington, DC. I was hired in 2020 to be the project manager for the grant-funded Libraries Build Business Initiative, and was thrilled to continue my work at PPA as a Deputy Director when the grant period ended. In my role, I co-lead our broadband and digital equity policy portfolio, with a focus on E-rate and other FCC programs. I also continue leading our economic opportunity work, building upon the lessons learned and resources developed as part of the Libraries Build Business program.

Question 2: Your edited book on Libraries that *Build Business: Advancing Small Business and Entrepreneurship and in Public Libraries (2022)* is such a great resource for public libraries looking to explore, expand, and advocate for small businesses and entrepreneurship programs in their communities. Based on this work where you reviewed 26 case studies and profiles, are

there high level activities that public libraries are doing to support these areas and common challenges that you see what they are experiencing?
Megan: I enjoyed developing the book alongside all the chapter authors and contributors so much! The book includes case studies from twenty-six public libraries, as well as insights from other library types in the beginning chapters. We did our best to include public libraries from a wide range of locations and geographies, library and community sizes, and focus areas with the goal of demonstrating that any library, no matter their size or budget, can support small businesses and entrepreneurs.

In fact, I think many libraries already have the services and resources available that small business owners need: meeting space, Internet access, printers and copiers, software like Adobe, and books and databases. Many public libraries are working with community partners, like SCORE or small business development centers (SBDCs), to offer classes and workshops; offering one-to-one reference appointments with librarians to do market research and learn about the library's resources; and providing equipment and meeting space. These kinds of opportunities are critical to creating a thriving, equitable local economy as it allows individuals to test out their business ideas without upfront costs.

Partnerships are an important building block for offering programs and getting the word out, but they can be tricky to navigate. The book offers various tips and suggestions for navigating partnerships that are mutually beneficial and build capacity. Another big challenge is awareness about all that the library offers, so outreach and communication are also super important to build into programs. We have a free *Libraries Build Business Communications Toolkit* to support libraries with messaging, marketing, and basic advocacy for this reason.

Question 3: Your book is focused on public libraries and we wanted to ask for your thoughts on academic libraries like community colleges and their roles in supporting workforce developments in the communities they serve? Have you seen or heard of academic libraries supporting workforce development whether that is internally with career services centers or in partnership with public libraries? If so, can you talk about them or share your thoughts?
Megan: Absolutely, academic libraries have an important role to play and are doing great work in their communities and with students, faculty, and staff. I'll share just a couple of quick examples from Libraries Build Business, but ALA's Business Reference and Services Section (BRASS) is a great resource for more information about academic (and public) libraries supporting business. From Libraries Build Business, the Laramie County Library System in Wyoming partnered with the University of Wyoming library system to develop their statewide Library to Business initiative. The University provided a model, as well as technical assistance, for the business studios and stations that were developed in county libraries across the state. In Independence, Kansas, the

Independence Public Library offered a small makerspace for business owners that included a laser engraver, a large-format printer, and access to the Adobe Creative Cloud. For access to additional equipment and studio space, trainings, and expertise, the library referred patrons to partners at the Independence Community College Center for Innovation and Entrepreneurship.

I had the great fortune of seeing both these programs in action, touring both the public libraries and their academic library counterparts in the last couple of years. These relationships are just so cool and open doors for everyone involved, making resources more accessible, better used, and allowing both public libraries and academic libraries to do what they do best.

Question 4: What are some areas regarding emerging technologies like AI that might support or challenge public libraries supporting workforce development? In our book, we have highlighted a few public libraries offering generative AI tool workshops for career development. We wanted to ask for your take on this topic and whether there is promise in generative AI tools in libraries supporting these areas?

Megan: Libraries are definitely thinking and talking about this as it relates to workforce and small business development! We just had an informal Libraries Build Business discussion about how libraries are thinking about incorporating generative AI tools into their workforce and career development services. For any career, being digitally literate and digitally resilient is critical. Importantly, the library is a place where the public will go to learn about these technologies and get familiar with how to use them. For AI, part of that training and literacy will be helping people to understand the strengths and weaknesses of the technology to leverage it most effectively.

Question 5: Can you tell us the importance of advocacy work in securing funding for these library projects especially related to workforce development? What are strategies for libraries in speaking with stakeholders about the importance of libraries supporting small business owners, entrepreneurs and the economy?

Megan: Advocacy is vital to the sustainability and success of your library programs, but it doesn't have to be a big, scary thing. Advocacy is about strong communication and building relationships. You want people to know about your work, and to be excited about your work. The Libraries Build Business Communications Toolkit I mentioned earlier includes materials for libraries to talk with stakeholders across their ecosystems—other library staff and administration, community partners, small business owners, and elected officials and decision-makers. It is so critical that libraries are having these conversations at all levels—inviting local elected officials to events at the library, sending along good news about program impact, or sharing plans for future programs. The good work speaks for itself—simply sharing information about all the resources and programs the library provides, feedback from program participants, and making the work visible across the community will help. And our toolkit has templates and talking points to get started with presentations, emails, flyers, and other communications. Many libraries find that it's about consistency—keep showing up, become a familiar face, and invite people to be part of what you're working on. Your enthusiasm and collaborative spirit will go a long way. and PPA is here to help! We love good news stories that we can share with decision-makers, and we'd be glad to amplify your work, provide resources for your conversations and meetings, and generally be a partner.

In particular, everybody is excited about economic development and small business success, so these stories are effective and exciting to all kinds of stakeholders.

Question 6: Anything else you'd like to mention that we did not get to talk about?
Megan: Thank you again for this conversation. I would just reiterate that libraries are already doing this great work in big and small ways. The book offers tips and advice on developing partnerships, doing outreach, and tailoring your small business services to the needs of your community. The best part about the book is that the chapters are authored by library workers across the country that are engaged in doing this work in real time. They are our peers and colleagues in the field and you can reach out to them to learn more and work alongside them. Libraries Build Business has a community of practice where people share resources, challenges, and ideas and we move forward together, advancing libraries and further supporting thriving local economies and communities where people want to live and work. Workforce and economic development work will necessarily look different in every context, but there are tons of ideas out there to adapt and try, while considering the unique needs of your locale.

An Interview with Dr. Corinthia Price, Founder and CEO Workforce Career Readiness

Question 1: Thank you for speaking with us! Can you tell us about your role? How did you envision Workforce Career Readiness? How do you support career-seeking community members?
Corinthia: My name is Dr. Corinthia Price. I am the Founder and CEO of Workforce Career Readiness. Our goal at "Workforce Career Readiness" is to ensure that employees are equipped with the knowledge and skills necessary for success in a twenty-first-century marketplace. It is our firm belief here at Workforce Career Readiness that this will ensure that businesses and organizations have a competent workforce prepared to compete and thrive globally. We at WCR, specialize in preparing graduates to enter college, postsecondary training, and the workforce with both the attitude and the skills needed to

succeed and excel. I support career-seeking community members by providing resources, guidance, and opportunities to help them achieve their short-term employment and long-term career goals.

Question 2: What is a tool (or tools) that you commonly refer to or use?
Corinthia: Mentoring and coaching are valuable tools for skill development. Mentoring involves pairing less experienced individuals with more experienced professionals who can provide guidance, advice, and support. Through regular interactions and feedback, mentees can learn from their mentors' expertise and experience, helping them develop new skills and navigate their career paths more effectively. Coaching assists individuals in recognizing their strengths and weaknesses, setting goals, and devising strategies to enhance their performance. They may come from diverse backgrounds, regardless of the industry of the individuals being coached.

Work-based learning is another tool for skill development. Programs that integrate classroom learning with real-world work experience, such as internships, apprenticeships, and cooperative education programs. These programs utilize hands-on learning approaches to allow individuals to apply their knowledge in practical settings and gain valuable on-the-job training.

Question 3: How do you engage with your learners on career research or education?
Corinthia: Engaging learners in career research or education can be highly beneficial for their personal and professional development. Here are some effective strategies to engage with learners:

Guest speakers—Invite professionals from various industries to speak to your learners about their career paths and experiences. This can provide valuable insights and inspiration.

Career fairs—Organize a career fair where learners can interact with representatives from different companies and educational institutions. This can help them explore various options and make informed decisions about their future.

Workshops and seminars—Conduct workshops and seminars on topics such as resume writing, interview skills, and career planning. This can help learners develop important skills and knowledge for their future careers.

Networking opportunities—Provide opportunities for learners to network with professionals in their field of interest. This can help them build valuable connections and learn more about potential career paths.

Technology—Use technology to enhance the learning experience, such as online career assessments, virtual job shadowing, and Career Exploration Tools. This can help learners explore a wide range of career options from anywhere.

By using these strategies, you can effectively engage with your learners on career research and education, helping them make knowledgeable decisions about their future careers.

Question 4: What is often the most common issue that students experience when it comes to career research/education?
Corinthia: One of the most common issues that students experience when it comes to career research and education is a lack of direction. Many students are unsure about what career path to pursue or what steps to take to achieve their career goals. This can lead to feelings of confusion, indecision, and anxiety about the future.

Additionally, students may struggle to find reliable information about different career options or educational pathways. The rapidly changing marketplace and the wide range of career choices available can make it difficult for students to navigate their options and make informed decisions.

Another common issue is a lack of exposure to real-world experiences and opportunities. Students may not have access to internships, apprenticeships, mentorship programs, or other hands-on learning experiences that can help them explore their interests and gain valuable skills.

Finally, students may face barriers such as financial constraints or limited access to educational resources and support services. These barriers can make it challenging for students to pursue their educational and career goals.

Addressing these challenges requires providing students with comprehensive career exploration resources, opportunities for self-reflection and assessment, access to mentorship and guidance, and support in developing decision-making skills. Encouraging students to explore their interests, gain hands-on experience through internships or job shadowing, and seek out diverse perspectives can also help them navigate the complexities of career research and education more effectively.

Question 5: What are some trends in skill development or workforce development do you see?
Corinthia: Since the onset of the pandemic, we have been facing a talent shortage due to the enormous skills gap, which makes skills and workforce development initiatives imperative. There has been a swift progression in upskilling or reskilling how individuals work and the nature of the work within the labor market. Upskilling and reskilling are pivotal aspects of workforce development, particularly in response to evolving job demands and technological advancements. Upskilling involves enhancing existing skills to align with changing industry needs, while reskilling involves acquiring entirely new skills to transition into different roles or industries. Both practices are essential for individuals to remain competitive in the job market and for organizations to adapt to shifting skill requirements. Several trends are reshaping skill and workforce development.

Remote Work Skills—With the rise of remote work, skills related to remote collaboration, communication, and digital tools are in high demand.

Foundational Digital Literacy and Technology Skills—As technology continues to advance, skills in areas such as coding, data analysis, AI, and cybersecurity are increasingly important across various industries.

Soft Skills—Soft skills like communication, emotional intelligence, and problem-solving are gaining more recognition as essential for success in the workplace, especially as automation increases.

Diversity, Equity, and Inclusion (DEI) Training—There's a growing emphasis on DEI training to create more inclusive workplaces and address issues related to bias, discrimination, and inequality.

Green Skills—With increasing awareness of environmental issues, there's a growing demand for skills related to sustainability, renewable energy, and environmental conservation across various sectors.

Entrepreneurial Skills—Entrepreneurial skills such as creativity, innovation, risk-taking, and business acumen are valued not only by aspiring entrepreneurs but also by employees within organizations seeking to foster an entrepreneurial culture.

Health and Wellness—Employers are recognizing the importance of supporting employees' mental and physical health. As a result, there's a growing demand for skills related to stress management, mindfulness, and workplace wellness programs.

Global Competence—In an interconnected world, skills related to In an interconnected world, skills related to cultural humility, global communication, and working in diverse teams are increasingly valuable, especially for companies operating internationally.

Question 6: What are the opportunities and challenges for libraries in supporting these trends?
Corinthia: Libraries can be a powerful partner for upskilling and reskilling patrons. Libraries play a crucial role in supporting skill and workforce development trends, but they also face several opportunities and challenges in doing so.

<u>Opportunities:</u>
Access to Resources: Libraries offer access to a wide range of educational resources, including books, online courses, databases, and workshops, which can support skill development across various fields.

Community Engagement: Libraries serve as community hubs where people can gather for learning and networking opportunities. They can organize events, seminars, and skill-building workshops to engage and empower community members.

Technology Access: Libraries have long been leaders in digital inclusion. Many libraries provide access to computers, Internet connectivity, and digital tools, bridging the digital divide and enabling individuals to acquire digital literacy and tech skills necessary for today's workforce.

Partnerships: Libraries can collaborate with local businesses, educational institutions, nonprofits, and government agencies to offer specialized training and job shadowing programs, job fairs, and mentorship opportunities, expanding their capacity to support workforce development initiatives.

Challenges:
Funding: Many libraries face financial challenges, limiting their ability to invest in new technology, resources, and staff training necessary to support evolving skill development needs effectively.

Digital Transformation: While libraries strive to adapt to the digital age, the rapid pace of technological change presents challenges in terms of acquiring, staffing, maintaining, and providing access to digital resources and services.

Relevance and Visibility: Libraries must continuously demonstrate their relevance and value in supporting skill and workforce development to attract users and secure funding. This requires effective marketing, outreach efforts, and partnerships with relevant stakeholders.

Equity and Inclusion: Ensuring equitable access to resources and services is a significant challenge for libraries, particularly in underserved communities where individuals may face barriers such as lack of transportation, language barriers, or limited digital literacy skills.

Keeping Pace with Trends: Libraries need to stay informed about emerging skill development trends and the workforce needs to tailor their offerings effectively. This requires ongoing staff training, professional development, and strategic planning to remain responsive to changing demands.

Despite these challenges, libraries have a unique opportunity to serve as vital community hubs for skill and workforce development, economic empowerment, and social inclusion. By leveraging their strengths and addressing key challenges, libraries can continue to play a central role in supporting individuals' career aspirations and economic sustainability.

Question 7: What advice do you have for libraries supporting students who are job seekers or career education/research?
Corinthia: Libraries play a critical role in assisting students who are seeking employment or pursuing career education and research. Here are some valuable tips for libraries to enhance their services:

Access to Career Resources—Ensure that students have access to a wide range of career resources, including books, online databases, and websites that offer information on resumes, cover letters, job search strategies, and career exploration.

Workshops and Training—Offer workshops and training sessions on essential job search skills, such as resume writing, interview preparation, networking, and using online job search platforms.

Mock Interviews—Offer opportunities for students to participate in mock interviews to practice their interview skills and receive constructive feedback from library staff or volunteers.

Networking Events—Host networking events or career fairs where students can connect with employers, alumni, and professionals in their field of interest.

Career Counseling Services—Offer one-on-one career counseling services where students can receive personalized guidance and advice on their job search and career goals.

Online Resources—Curate a list of online resources and databases that students can access remotely for career research, job listings, industry trends, and professional development opportunities.

Question 8: Anything else you like to talk about that we did not get to discuss?

Corinthia: In closing, I would like to say that I believe that entrepreneurship is another important key to long-term economic stability. Starting a business is a challenging endeavor that takes persistence, tenacity, and stick-to-itiveness. Libraries have long been a hub for workshops, seminars, and resources to assist those who decide to become business owners. Many times, at those workshops and seminars there are golden opportunities for individuals to meet and talk to people who have tried, failed, and tried again to start businesses. Libraries can readily provide information about where to go to get connected with vital resources like the Small Business Administration (SBA) and local Chambers of Commerce. Libraries are also excellent places to find out how to get certified as a Minority and/or Women-owned Business Enterprise (MWBE). Additionally, those looking for information about grants for small businesses and start-ups can access a wealth of information easily in their local or academic library.

CHAPTER SUMMARY

Promoting what your library is doing supporting workforce development can increase funding resources. Connecting to advocacy work at the global level, regional level, and national level can demonstrate library's relevancy and connection supporting economy, job seekers, and community. This chapter highlighted programs nationally and globally and focused on future workforce trends and opportunities for planning purposes. Advocacy work within the library field is critical and continues to demonstrate impact and value.

NOTES

1. Koop, Avery, and Bhabna Banerjee. "Mapped: Unemployed Workers vs. Job Openings by U.S. State." August 3, 2023. Accessed at https://www.visualcapitalist.com/unemployed-workers-vs-job-openings-by-us-state/.

2. Ibid.
3. World Economic Forum. "The Future of Jobs Report 2023." April 30, 2023. Accessed at https://www.weforum.org/publications/the-future-of-jobs-report-2023/#:~:text=The%20Future%20of%20Jobs%20Report%202023%20explores%20how%20jobs%20and,the%20workplace%20of%20the%20future.
4. World Economic Forum. "Future of Jobs Report 2023 Insight Report." May 2023, p. 36. Accessed at https://www3.weforum.org/docs/WEF_Future_of_Jobs_2023.pdf.
5. Marr, Bernard. "The Top 10 In-Demand Skills for 2023." *Forbes*, February 14, 2023. Accessed at https://www.forbes.com/sites/bernardmarr/2023/02/14/the-top-10-in-demand-skills-for-2030/?sh=794912582fb9.
6. U.S. Bureau of Labor Statistics. "Occupational Outlook Handbook: Fastest Growing Occupations." Accessed at https://www.bls.gov/ooh/fastest-growing.htm.
7. National Skills Coalition. "LinkedIn." Accessed at https://www.linkedin.com/company/nationalskillscoalition/?miniCompanyUrn=urn%3Ali%3Afs_miniCompany%3A2592383.
8. Kear, Robin, and Loida Garcia-Febo. "ALA UN 2030 Sustainable Development Goals Task Force." *International Journal of Librarianship*, vol. 5, no. 2 (2020): 95. https://doi.org/10.23974/ijol.2020.vol5.2.173.
9. United Nations Department of Economic and Social Affairs Sustainable Development. "Goal 8: Promote Sustained, Inclusive and Sustainable Economic Growth, Full and Productive Employment and Decent Work for All." Accessed at https://sdgs.un.org/goals/goal8.
10. Webb, Amy. "How to Prepare for a GenAI Future You Can't Predict." *Harvard Business Review*, August 31, 2023. Accessed at https://hbr.org/2023/08/how-to-prepare-for-a-genai-future-you-cant-predict?ab=HP-hero-featured-text-1.
11. Lucas, Emmy. "Five AI Tools To Help With Your Job Search—Or With Helping You Quit." *Forbes*, July 17, 2023. Accessed at https://www.forbes.com/sites/emmylucas/2023/07/17/five-ai-tools-to-help-with-your-job-search-or-with-helping-you-quit/?sh=322e5b0e372c.
12. Park, Eugenie, and Risa Gelles-Watnick. "Most Americans Haven't Used ChatGPT; Few Think it Will Have a Major Impact on Their Job." *Pew Research Center*, August 28, 2023. Accessed at https://www.pewresearch.org/short-reads/2023/08/28/most-americans-havent-used-chatgpt-few-think-it-will-have-a-major-impact-on-their-job/.
13. Ibid.
14. American Library Association. "Advocacy Action Planning." Accessed at https://www.ala.org/advocacy/advocacy-action-planning.
15. Redwood City Library Foundation. "How the Makerspace Helped Launch a New Career." November 16, 2023. Accessed at https://www.rclfdn.org/post/how-the-makerspace-helped-launch-a-new-career-1?utm_campaign=31c4234c-6df0-415d-884d-9f402f17706c&utm_source=so&utm_medium=mail&cid=9c95cee4-de03-4d77-8f2b-d4291220e3d8.
16. Winning Elections & Influencing Politicians for Library Funding, 2017, 60.
17. The White House. "Preparing Our Country for a Cyber Future: National Cyber Workforce and Education Strategy & Implementation." Accessed at https://www.whitehouse.gov/oncd/preparing-our-country-for-a-cyber-future/.

18. Awareness Days. "National Careers Week 2023." Accessed at https://www.awarenessdays.com/awareness-days-calendar/national-careers-week-2023/.
19. Urban Libraries Council. "Mission." Accessed at https://www.urbanlibraries.org/about/mission.
20. Urban Libraries Council. "2023 Innovations Winners Brochure." Accessed at https://www.urbanlibraries.org/files/2023-Innovations-Winners-Brochure.pdf.
21. https://www.urbanlibraries.org/initiatives/workforce-economic-developmentUrban Libraries Council. "Workforce & Economic Development." Accessed at https://www.urbanlibraries.org/initiatives/workforce-economic-development.
22. Urban Libraries Council. "Strengthening Libraries as Entrepreneurial Hubs." Accessed at https://www.urbanlibraries.org/initiatives/workforce-economic-development/strengthening-libraries-as-hubs-for-entrepreneurship.
23. Urban Libraries Council. "Business Value Calculator Early Results and Insights." Accessed at https://www.urbanlibraries.org/files/BVC-Early-Results-Report_2022_Final.pdf.
24. Quintana, Sergio, and Thom Jensen. "Vice President Kamala Harris Meets With Small Business Owners in SF's Chinatown." *NBC Bay Area*, March 3, 2023. Accessed at https://www.nbcbayarea.com/news/local/san-francisco/kamala-harris-san-francisco-chinatown/3171676/.
25. San Francisco Public Library. "MINUTES Council of Neighborhood Libraries March 23, 2023 4:00 p.m." Accessed at https://sfpl.org/sites/default/files/2023-06/M%203.23.23.pdf.
26. "Shifting Library Staff Perspectives on Supporting Entrepreneurship: Caitlyn Tipps (Plano Public Lib)." Entrepreneurship & Libraries Conference. Accessed at https://www.youtube.com/watch?v=vNaSOqNP_6I&list=PPSV.
27. Kyaw, Arrman. "CUNY Launches $16 Million Public-Private Partnership to Improve Student Career Success and Bolster Economic Growth." *Diverse Education*, September 22, 2022. https://www.diverseeducation.com/students/article/15297104/cuny-launches-16-million-publicprivate-partnership-to-improve-student-career-success-and-bolster-economic-growth.
28. Brooklyn College. "Jobs & Careers: Home." Accessed at https://libguides.brooklyn.cuny.edu/jobscareers.
29. Fried, Michael. "Understanding the Impact of Work-Based Learning." Accessed at https://sr.ithaka.org/blog/understanding-the-impact-of-work-based-learning/.
30. AAC&U. "Trending Topic: High Impact Practices." Accessed at https://www.aacu.org/trending-topics/high-impact.
31. McKay, H.D. "Supporting the Career Outcomes of Professional Programs: The Relevance of Portfolios and Case Studies for Masters of Marketing Students in Their Job Search." *Academic BRASS*, vol. 18, no. 1 (Spring 2023). Accessed at https://www.ala.org/rusa/sites/ala.org.rusa/files/content/sections/brass/Publications/Acad_BRASS/2023_spring_McKay.pdf.
32. Ibid.
33. AACSB. "Business Accreditation." Accessed at https://www.aacsb.edu/educators/accreditation/business-accreditation.
34. Reference and User Services Association (RUSA), a Division of the American Library Association. "Guidelines for Business Information Responses." Accessed at https://www.ala.org/rusa/resources/guidelines/business.

35. Erntrelib Entrepreneurship & Libraries Conference. "Fall 2023: Refresh & Refocus: Libraries' New Trends in Supporting Entrepreneurship." Accessed at https://entrelib.org/fall-2023/.
36. Maine Department of Economic & Community Development. "Maine State Library and Department of Economic and Community Development Announce $1.7M in Maine Jobs & Recovery Plan Grants to Support Remote Work at Local Libraries." August 3, 2023. Accessed at https://www.maine.gov/decd/about/news/maine-state-library-and-department-economic-and-community-development-announce-17m-maine.

4

Resources and Training

This chapter covers:

- Theories, resources, and organizations for supporting career development and workforce program.
- Professional development training for supporting career development.

In this chapter, we examine resources, tools, and training that will support libraries in developing services and programs related to career services, workforce development, and entrepreneurship. We examine definitions and keywords as well as theories on this topic as well. A lot of these resources are free which means that if there are library workers interested in this work, they may find these resources to be useful in developing their professional work and interest. We also examine the conferences and workshops that are held virtually and on-site that might offer professional learning regardless of library type.

ADULT LEARNING THEORIES

When thinking about engaging in the work for career services support within the academic library, it is important to think about traditional and nontraditional students. Nontraditional students may be adult learners who may be older and have different life experiences from traditional students. When thinking about adult learners, adult learning theories come into play. It is important to think about how to apply such theories into practice or to incorporate into your services and approach. Advocating for adult learners requires you to think about services that may customize and support their learning needs (Knowles, 1984). Here are some points about adult learners:

A Preference for Self-Directed Learning

- Drawing on life experience to assist with learning
- Readiness to learn centered on the performance of social functions
- Applying new knowledge to real-life situations and problems
- A tendency to be internally motivated

These areas might help you rethink how to engage with learners who might need to consider other aspects such as their own experiences or learning how to apply new knowledge in real situations. This may mean setting up asynchronous courses, meeting with users in person or online and asking them to reflect on their lived experiences and past work experiences, and offering resources for them to explore and feel empowered. Of course, not everyone can relate with these experiences but they may help frame some of the work you are doing when thinking about serving adult learners.

For more information on adult learning theories, consider exploring online classes like Coursera. Coursera offers online classes as part of Goodwill® Career Coach and Navigator Professional Certificate such as Foundations of Career Navigating and Coaching (fifteen hours), which gets into several adult learning theories such as Maslow Hierarchy of Needs.[1] Completing the class or certificate program can support you to prepare your services and resources to meet your job seekers and their needs while also understanding external factors that may impact their progress such as issues in housing, elder/child care, skill-building, and so forth. We recommend you to explore these courses and understand how to best prepare services or to enhance the existing services you offer already in your libraries. The adult learning theories will help you think about applying learning theories into your services that will enhance your job seekers' experiences.

For this section, we divide this list into classes and resources, which may include podcasts, readings, and external organizations to look into.

PROFESSIONAL DEVELOPMENT TRAINING AND RESOURCES

Sharing Resources and Referral Processes

Some organizations have offered workshops to convene with partners to prepare for a community of job seekers in a collaborative environment. For example, the Portage Area Workforce Service Connection was established in 2020 by Chris Baker, Public Library Consultant, Library Services Team from Wisconsin Department of Public Instruction, and Mark Jochem, Workforce Development Consultant from South Central Library System in Wisconsin to establish a "referral network," where they identified and convened a meeting with relevant and potential community organizations to support job seekers.[2]

This approach helps reduce duplicative efforts, raise awareness of each organization's work and efforts on workforce development, highlight and boost social services, and create a centralized location of resources and partners for the library and for agencies involved. By offering workshops to bring partners together to brainstorm and think about their strengths and challenges, the library can position itself as a community leader in connecting resources and partnerships in a facilitated discussion.[3]

If you are looking to train community partners and inform them about training resources, consider the SkillsCommon Repository [https://www.skillscommons.org/]. This open educational resource focuses on vocational education materials. Bringing in workforce training materials for a range of careers, SkillsCommon is funded by the U.S. Department of Labor and is managed by the California State University Long Beach and MERLOT with more than 700 institutions contributing training resources in a variety of industries from construction to healthcare to technologies.

Building Collections: We decided not to list book titles here because there are numerous publications on resume and cover letter writing, career development, and management that you can search for and these publications tend to be outdated after a while.

- You may consider offering these lists of serial publications in your collections or refer to them in your online guide/flyer since some do not allow free access: *Forbes Magazine, Inc. Magazine, Fast Company, Harvard Business Review*, and *The Wall Street Journal.*
- For databases, we recommended several based on specialties in chapter 2 for teaching purposes. Databases and their titles/collections also change often based on the vendor. As of December 2023, here are some additional ones to consider:
  - **Career & Technical Education Database (Proquest):** Vocational information on technical topics, such as computing science, healthcare, building trades, auto mechanics, sales and retail, accounting, graphic design, and photography.
  - **Vocational & Career Collection (EBSCO):** Covers trade and industry-related periodicals.
  - **Associations Unlimited (Gale):** International and U.S. national, regional, state, and local nonprofit membership organizations in all fields.

Building any library collection (print or digital) can take time to promote and assess. If you incorporate them in your teaching or training demos, it can be a useful resource not only to your job seekers but to the partners you refer to. They can recommend these resources as needed. Most importantly, most of these databases are not free so you will need to be strategic on what you collect and how you assess them if your collection budget is limited. Consider reviewing the *NASIG Core Competencies for Electronic Resources Librarians* to understand the life cycles of e-resources.[4]

Classes and Conferences

Coursera: Introduction to Career Coach and Navigator Professional Certificate—this online certificate program is "part of Goodwill® Career Coach and Navigator Professional Certificate."[5] There are four modules in this program:

1. Introduction to career coaching and navigating
2. Theories behind career coaching and navigating
3. Client relationship management
4. Human-centered navigating and coaching

Once you complete this course, you will receive a professional certificate that highlights the concepts, foundation understanding, and skills needed to better support job seekers as career navigators, which plays an important role to connect and support job seekers with appropriate resources, and skill-building training or education. This resource can be shared with colleagues who are starting this work.

National Career Development Association (NCDA) [https://www.ncda.org/] is "an organization that provides professional development, publications, standards, and advocacy to practitioners and educators who inspire and empower individuals to achieve their career and life goals."[6] NCDA also offers the Certified Career Services Provider (CCSP) "which is intended for providers offering career services in an array of roles and settings. Providers might be consultants, coaches, advisors, workforce practitioners, facilitators, trainers, recruiters, and resume writers."[7] This could be a useful training program that Lateka Grays from an interview in chapter 1 emphasized.

For certifications, if you are seeking associations that provide certification or training, the Career One Stop's Professional Association Finder can help identify organizations that certifies training in supporting career development.[8] Credential Finder is another resource to search for educational and career pathways across universities, colleges, and institutions.[9] CAEL "is a national nonprofit that supports the creation of education-to-career pathways, fueling economic mobility and community prosperity for all"[10] and offers an online course called, "Career and Education Advising Course." This fee-based 12-week online course highlights career development theory to the student's work and offers training and resources to develop education training. Here are the other areas it covers

- Apply career development theory to your work
- Advising Adults: Approaches and competencies
- Exploring career and education options

- Advising Diverse Populations: understanding social, cultural, and economic contexts
- Advise a diverse workforce
- The Career Planning Process: assessment, data-gathering, goal-setting, and action plan
- Ethics in advising
- Capstone: You will be required to exhibit understanding of the skills necessary for providing a successful career and education advising.[11]

These online workforce/career services workshops may be helpful in expanding your services, training your colleagues, or offering a new perspective on workforce development programs.

For libraries focusing on workforce development, consider training and courses from the ALA, PLA, Infopeople, Library Juice Academy, and Amigos Library Services for online learning. Periodically these courses will come up to support libraries' workforce development and entrepreneurship efforts.

For example, Amigos Library Services offered this online class, "Entrepreneurial: Supporting Small Business Development in Libraries" taught by Erin Gray in 2024,

> Libraries are dynamic hubs of innovation and support for local entrepreneurs and small business owners. Empower librarians and library staff to play a vital role in the growth and success of their local small business communities. Connect library users to resources from business plans to licensing and business marketing.[12]

Learning objectives for this session include:

- Understanding the needs and challenges of entrepreneurs
- Developing programs for new and established small business owners
- Supporting community startup initiatives[13]

We anticipate that more training and classes will be offered because workforce development and entrepreneurship programs are critical to the community and the library plays a vital role in supporting economic development. In addition, there are other programs available such as the Compassionate Career Services, a series in 2021 led by librarians Djaz Zulida, Shauna Edson, and Ricci Yuhico. The speakers shared best practices in engaging with job seekers. This series is provided by METRO, which is a nonprofit service provider that helps libraries, archives, and museums in New York City and Westchester County and covers areas on supporting job seekers experiencing technology issues and libraries needing to offer social services or reframe how they provide training and support.

Resources and Training

- Part I: Providing Assistance to Those Who Benefit Most[14]
- Part II: Tips and Tricks for Working Across the Digital Divide[15]
- Part III: When and How to "Teach People to Fish"[16]

Part III is especially helpful for those who may be experienced and may experience burnout in the process of supporting job seekers.

Another free webinar series is from the PLA and Libswork, a national networking group supporting workforce and small business development, "Partnering to Meet Community Workforce Needs" presented by Larra Clark, Scott B. Sanders, Shayne Spaulding, Xenia Hernández, and Shanika Wallace.[17] Here are other one in the series and the presenters:

- Strengthen Patron Workforce Opportunities with Labor Market Information Panelists: Stephanie Holcomb, David Klokner, Ron Painter, and Natalie Ruppert.
- Supporting Patrons to Obtain In-Demand Credentials That Boost Employability and Career Mobility Panelists: Emily Felt, Haley Glover, Karsten Heise, Elizabeth Iaukea, and Tammy Westergard.
- Bridging Workers' Digital Skills Gaps through Libraries Panelists: Stacey Aldrich, Amanda Bergson-Shilcock, Scott Kuchinsky, Jen Nelson, and Ka'ala Souza.
- Boosting Youth Workforce Readiness Panelists: Kate Aubin, Janelle Duray, Marquita Friday, and Jennifer Griffin.
- Supporting Formerly Incarcerated Individuals with a Fresh Start @ Your Library Panelists: Sherry Sandler, Sarah Swiderski, and Nicole Warren.

For those interested in entrepreneurship and libraries, consider the Entrepreneurship Libraries Conference [ELC] held free and virtually annually.

The ELC offers free online conferences and workshops on how libraries and librarians can support entrepreneurship in their communities and campuses. ELC leadership includes a diverse mix of public, special, and academic librarians and partners, from several countries. The ELC is for and by information professionals who support and believe in the power of inquiry and information to transform lives and support entrepreneurial endeavors.[18]

Some of the past conferences focused on building workforce development programs, business research, data literacy, and more. These sessions are recorded and available on the website at https://entrelib.org/.

Resources, Readings, and Podcasts

Courses are generally structured to engage in your learning through a variety of resources. However, there are additional resources such as readings and podcasts to explore on this topic. Here is a sample of resources that we wanted to highlight for you to explore:

LibsWork—Libraries Work [To subscribe, visit https://database.mail-list.com/app/subscribe?ln=libswork and to post: libswork-list-owner@lists.lib.wa.us] is a discussion group list focusing on libraries and workforce development. They hold meetings virtually and open to all public libraries, consortium, and state libraries to participate in these national discussions and to share resources and programs. We highly recommend you join this listserv to view and participate in these conversations known as LibsWork Lounge.

In addition, here are other listservs to consider exploring, which may include updates and information regarding career services/workforce development and advocacy work. and some may require membership to join:

- Association of College and Research Libraries [https://www.ala.org/acrl/aboutacrl/listserv]
- PLA [https://www.ala.org/pla/about/connect]
- Reference and User Services Association (RUSA) BRASS [https://www.ala.org/rusa/sections/brass/involved]. We will explore more on BRASS resources in the next section of this chapter.
- ALA [https://www.ala.org/pla/advocacy]
- American Library Association Allied Professional Association (ALA-APA) [https://ala-apa.org/newsletter/]
- BUSLIB-L [BUSLIB-L@LISTS.NAU.EDU] "is a listserv where business librarians from special, academic, and public libraries of all sizes, corporate information professionals, information product and services vendors, and anybody else can ask business reference-related questions and share their expertise. Search online archives for background information."[19] There are resources and webinars often shared related to small business developments, research, and entrepreneurship through this listserv. There are also complex business research questions from students, faculty, or researchers posed and responded by members of the listserv. The listserv is free and open to all to join!

National Association of Colleges and Employers (NACE), "an American nonprofit professional association . . . for college career services, recruiting practitioners, and others who wish to hire the college educated,"[20] recently released a report based on a research survey on "the Class of 2022 Employment Rate Matched Pre-Pandemic Level." These reports from NACE can offer insights on how to plan and prepare career services collaboratively within higher education or in public libraries. Consider signing up for their NACE Insights newsletters for updates.

Career One Stop [https://www.careeronestop.org/] is another important resource to explore and recommend job seekers. "CareerOneStop is the flagship career, training, and job search website for the U.S. Department of Labor. The website serves job seekers, businesses, students, and career advisors with a variety of free online tools, information and resources."[21] Consider signing up for their Connections newsletter for updates.

National Skills Coalition (NSC) [https://nationalskillscoalition.org/], as mentioned earlier, NSC is an organization that "organizes broad-based coalitions seeking to raise the skills of America's workers across a range of industries"[22] is another great resource to explore for partnerships, ideas, and ways to support skills for employment purposes. Sign up for their newsletters/mailing list for updates. In March 2021, NSC hosted a webinar called, "Libraries and Workforce Development: Connecting the Dots between Your Patrons and Public Policy."[23] The one-hour webinar focused on federal policies supporting workforce development and how libraries can align and support these efforts. Amanda Bergson-Shilcock, Senior Fellow, and Jessica Cardott, Former Senior National Network Manager, presented skill-building opportunities for public libraries regarding economic development and recovery. This webinar is part of a series of events regarding public libraries and workforce development.

Workforce Monitor [WFM] [https://wfmonitor.com/]—this organization

> publishes report summaries and explanatory feature articles about workforce development. Launched in 2021 by veteran education writer and journalist George Lorenzo, WFM's overall mission is to synthesize information in a format that gets quickly to what matters most without any fluff and distracting advertisements that interrupt a reader's flow.[24]

You can subscribe to the WFM newsletter to get workforce development updates from an educational perspective from community college programs to policy implications. One notable article is the "non-degree credential quality imperative" and how "non-degree credentials are currently being analyzed by policy makers and workforce trainers and developers at the state level."[25] This information can be examined by a career services/workforce development librarian to partner with agencies to offer non-degree credentials based on recommendations or effectiveness of these programs.

WorkingNation [https://workingnation.com/]—a nonprofit media organization covering the future work—offers videos, podcasts, opinions, commentaries, reports, and news about workforce development trends and issues. We recommend exploring this site to learn more about changes happening in the job market across sectors.

Articles and Texts Worth Exploring

New business librarians and onboarding: For new business librarians in academic or public libraries, consider reading this article to support onboarding process:

Hess, S. F. & Mahoney, M. & Nicolosi, G. & Zabel, D., (2023) "Q1 and Then Some: Onboarding New Academic Business Librarians", *Ticker: The Academic Business Librarianship Review* 8(1). doi: https://doi.org/10.3998/ticker.4468

This article dives into what business librarians should know to prepare their work supporting business researchers. This article can also be useful for those thinking about getting into workforce development and business librarianship but not sure how to start.

Measures that Matter [https://measuresthatmatter.net/] is a project report that is worth exploring. This project is from the Chief Officers of State Library Agencies known as COSLA and in partnership with the Institute of Museum and Library Services (IMLS) to "examine, evaluate, and map the landscape of public library data collection in the United States."[26] One project is called "Public Libraries' Role in Workforce and Small Business Development" and offers case studies from libraries in San Diego to Asotin to Memphis across the United States. These libraries serve rural, suburban, and urban communities, and the case studies highlight assessments and data collection for impact regarding workforce development.

Data Literacy: As the workforce becomes and expects more data skills, we see the importance of libraries in supporting this area. You may want to read this article, especially for those in academic libraries and public libraries supporting training:

Pothier, W. & Condon, P. (2023) Cultivating a Data Literate Workforce: Considerations for Librarians.portal: Libraries and the Academy, Vol. 23, No. 4 (2023), pp. 629–636. https://scholars.unh.edu/faculty_pubs/1614/

Pothier and Condon examined the importance of data literacy in the workforce and what librarians can do to educate and train people. They found that "projections by Forrester Consulting, a global market research company, suggest that nearly 70 percent of the workforce would be expected to use data heavily in their work by 2025."[27] They also described how "employees can feel frustrated and find it challenging to manage the vast amount of data and information in their workload." They argued for a number of potential activities including the importance of partnerships between "higher education, professional organizations and industry," and "partnering with campus career services [for academic libraries] . . . to extend data literacy conversations with both internal and external audiences."[28] Data literacy becomes an increasingly important skill due to the integration of AI in the workplace.

Artificial Intelligence: We mentioned a lot about AI earlier regarding lesson plans and what libraries have been doing. We also recognize that the technology is changing and more tools will come out after this book has been published. AI will transform every sector from medical to legal to higher education. However, there will be a lot of articles regarding AI for business development but it is important to note the challenges as well. For example, Birdeye Blog's *14 Tools and 7 Strategies to Use AI for Small Business* by Shruti Dugar published in

October 2023[29] outlines ways for business owners to use AI for their development plan from marketing to translation work to financial analysis. It is meant to creatively inspire how AI can complement one's business.

One group to explore on this matter is the State Libraries and AI Technologies Working Group (SLAAIT). The working group is a "joint project of 14 state libraries to understand the opportunities, challenges, and risks associated with AI and the library sector."[30] Their work could be helpful for future libraries to consider on AI issues and workforce development. It is also important to note about privacy issues, data collection issues that select states may have legislation in place for businesses to comply with consumer data privacy laws.[31] So that means that if you offer to share this resource with your users who are business owners, they should be aware of these legislations. In addition, AI tools, especially new ones, are vulnerable to data breaching as OpenAI experienced this in March 2023.[32]

Library Associations and Resources:
Library Associations have offered numerous resources to explore. We highlight a few here that may be useful and relevant to your needs.

ALA released the Libraries that Build Business: *Advancing Small Business and Entrepreneurship in Public Libraries in 2022* and edited by Megan Janicki from the ALA Public Policy and Advocacy Office (see Megan's interview in chapter 3) and the *Libraries Build Business Playbook* in 2022, which is a great resource on how libraries can support small business and entrepreneurship in the communities.[33]

The PLA's "Public Library Staff and Diversity Report"[34] Survey in 2021 shared important details regarding staffing challenges and improving equity, diversity, and inclusion in the workplace. Be sure to explore this when you are thinking of ways to increase staffing positions for specific roles such as workforce development programs to better support your communities. We also talked about hiring bilingual librarians and librarians whose backgrounds reflect the diverse communities in previous chapters. It is important to see the national trends and issues through a survey like PLA. In addition, PLA offers support for public libraries in these areas as part of their initiatives:

- DigitalLearn.org
- DigitalLearn Tools for Trainers
- DigitalLearn for Rural Libraries
- Public WiFi Access Micro grants
- Skilling for Employment Post COVID-19.

The RUSA's BRASS has an abundance of information from newsletters to research guides to communities supporting business researchers and developments.

In the BRASS newsletter, a free digital newsletter, there are relevant articles such as a recent one, "Consulting Firm Whitepapers: A Must for a Business Researcher's Toolkit" by Susan M. Klopper published in 2023, vol 18, no. 2. Klopper explains who the consulting firms are, what whitepapers are, Google search strategies, and why use them. For example, like newspaper articles and reports, the whitepapers can provide

> [business] insight to corporate decision-making processes and the consumer journey. They are a must for interview preparation; they contain insights, data, and perspectives that can help distinguish students from others interviewing for an internship or job . . . .[35]

In another BRASS newsletter article entitled, "Business librarians' roles in supporting AACSB accreditation: A discussion about the potentials" by Grace Liu published in 2021, vol 16, no. 2, this article highlights how libraries can support the AACSB. Liu writes how she empowers students' career preparation with evidence-based career research by partnering with the career center. Students develop skills in finding information about career paths by major and prepare students for job interviews.[36] By exploring the BRASS newsletters, librarians may encounter useful tips and advice in supporting their researchers and job seekers.

Another useful BRASS resource is the "Guidelines for Business Information Responses," which is "designed to assist information services staff in meeting user needs to resolve business information inquiries, as developed by members of the American Library Association."[37] The guidelines offer guidance for librarians to understand their role in supporting users who are seeking business information.

Be sure to check your local/state/regional chapters, which may have a section supporting local business and entrepreneurship communities.

Podcast Conversations Worth Exploring

Public Libraries Online released a podcast episode called Workforce Development and features Larra Clark, PLA Deputy Director and ALA Public Policy & Advocacy and Natalie Ruppert, Manager, Career & Job Services Division at Kenton County (KY) Public Library. This episode is about twenty minutes long on SoundCloud, and both of them discuss PLA initiatives and engagement on workforce development such as the

> concept of career navigators and new research examining the role U.S. public libraries play in supporting workforce and small business development. The research, conducted by Measures that Matter, an initiative of Chief Officers of State Library Agencies [COSLA] in cooperation with Institute of Museum and Library Services [IMLS], provides an increased

understanding of current library practices and how they intersect with existing workforce systems and identifies challenges to data collection and outcome measurement.[38]

Take a moment to listen to this and get practice advice and examples from a librarian and from a library association.

In *Library Leadership Podcast,* Julie Brophy, Adult and Community Engagement Manager, Baltimore County Public Library (MD) speaks with Diane Luccy, Business and Careers Manager at the RIchland Library (SC) about libraries supporting economic development for their communities and the value of libraries as a resource for local business development. This episode is about twenty-eight minutes long, and Brophy asks important questions and ways to get started such as

> where is your place in the community? For that, you need to start by gathering information. This could include reviewing data on the type and number of local businesses and industries, identifying key stakeholders in the business community, and finding out what roles the municipal and county governments play in supporting local businesses.[39]

This conversation will help you think about the importance of libraries in supporting local economies.

In *Workforce Waves,* there is an episode called "How Libraries Help Job Seekers and Employers," which came out in March 2020.[40] In twenty-one minutes, Marne Martin, President of IFS's Service Management Business Unit and CEO of WorkWave speaks with three Wisconsin library system librarians Sherry Machones, Anne Hamland, and Leah Langby on ways libraries support workforce development. The conversation focuses on Libraries Activating Workforce Development Skills (LAWDS) project funded by the IMLS. LAWDS offer workshops, training, and meetings and to build relationships. The speakers discuss how to create a referral system and partnership with workforce development specialists. A common request from job seekers is looking for jobs and applying for jobs but they do not have an email address. They would need to create an email address and develop computer skills and then search and apply for jobs. Another common request is applying for unemployment benefits. Overall, this episode shares relevant examples and stories of libraries aligning with workforce development efforts. This podcast episode is especially useful for those who are not familiar with library resources supporting workforce development.

The Aspen Institute, a nonprofit committed to realizing a free, just, and equitable society, posts numerous free resources regarding local community engagement and programming. There are focused conversations on global and specialized topics that may serve as a resource for listeners, especially job seekers and those who support them. For example, in one podcast episode in November 2023 from "Aspen Ideas to Go" called "Work and Life Advice for the Nonlinear Path," which featured Bruce Feiler, an author and speaker, Kevin Kelly, Senior Maverick, Wired Magazine, and Joanne Lipman, a journalist and author.[41] In fifty-two minutes, this conversation centers on finding meaning in work and how careers and lives "are not linear" yet we have linear expectations of our careers. There are and will be life changes that disrupt work and career decisions. The speakers discuss changes in making choices when it comes to the career.

In another podcast conversation, "Investing in Shared American Prosperity" centers on economic hardship, transforming the economy, and the issues in global economy trends. This episode is about 48 minutes long and the guest speakers are Heather Boushey, Chief Economist, White House Invest in America Cabinet, Gene Ludwig, Founder and CEO, Ludwig Advisors, and Gillian Tett, Editorial Board Chair, *Financial Times*.[42] They get into government and economic policies in structuring, job creation, and global economy issues. These are big topics that may not be relevant to your local economy or interest but it is important to think about the implications of federal and state policies and market trends.

CHAPTER SUMMARY

This chapter highlights resources such as organizations, readings, adult learning theories, webinars, classes, podcasts, and guidelines for you to consider to explore for professional development and expand your practice supporting career services and workforce development programs. Being proactively engaged in this topic means that you have a variety of resources to support your learning in developing a robust workforce development program and career services to support your communities of users and their needs. We anticipate growing resources supporting economic, workforce, career, and business developments, and this is not meant to be an exhaustive list. We hope this will inspire you to explore these resources and share them with your colleagues.

NOTES

1. Coursera. "Foundations of Career Navigating and Coaching." Accessed at https://www.coursera.org/learn/foundations-of-career-navigating-and-coaching/home/welcome.
2. LibsWork Meeting. "The Center of the Spoke [Video]." December 12, 2023. Accessed at https://www.youtube.com/watch?v=8k_tvdgH7YM.
3. Portage Public Library. Accessed at https://www.portagelibrary.us/.
4. NASIG. "NASIG Core Competencies for Electronic Resources Librarians." Accessed at https://www.nasig.org/Competencies-Eresources.

5. Coursera. "Foundations of Career Navigating and Coaching." Accessed at https://www.coursera.org/learn/foundations-of-career-navigating-and-coaching/home/welcome.
6. National Career Development Association (NCDA). "Mission & Vision." Accessed at https://www.ncda.org/aws/NCDA/pt/sp/about.
7. National Career Development Association (NCDA). "Certified Career Services Provider (CCSP)." Accessed at https://www.ncda.org/aws/NCDA/pt/sp/credentialing_ccsp.
8. Career One Stop Business Center. "Professional Association Finder." Accessed at https://www.careeronestop.org/BusinessCenter/Toolkit/find-professional-associations.aspx.
9. Credential Finder. "Discover Credentials. Explore Opportunities." Accessed at https://credentialfinder.org/.
10. CAEL. "About Us: What We Do." Accessed at https://www.cael.org/about-us/what-we-do.
11. CAEL. "Career and Education Advising Course." Accessed at https://web.cvent.com/event/56a19093-2afd-4a41-ba40-a66f4ff72f45/summary.
12. Amigos Library Services. "Entrepreneurial: Supporting Small Business Development in Libraries." Accessed at https://www.amigos.org/civicrm/event/info%3Fid%3D2006%26amp%3Breset%3D1.
13. Amigos Library Services. "Entrepreneurial: Supporting Small Business Development in Libraries." Accessed at https://www.amigos.org/civicrm/event/info%3Fid%3D2006%26amp%3Breset%3D1.
14. Metropolitan New York Library Council. "Compassionate Career Services, Part One: Providing Assistance to Those Who Benefit Most [Video]." Accessed at https://metro.org/events/compassionate-career-services-part-one-providing-assistance-those-who-benefit-most.
15. Metropolitan New York Library Council. "Compassionate Career Services, Part Two: Tips and Tricks for Working Across the Digital Divide [Video]." Accessed at https://metro.org/events/compassionate-career-services-part-two-tips-and-tricks-working-across-digital-divide.
16. Metropolitan New York Library Council. "Compassionate Career Services, Part Three: When and How to Teach People to Fish [Video]." Accessed at https://metro.org/events/compassionate-career-services-part-three-when-and-how-teach-people-fish.
17. Public Library Association. "Partnering to Meet Community Workforce Needs [Video]." Accessed at https://www.ala.org/pla/education/onlinelearning/webinars/ondemand/partnering.
18. Erntrelib Entrepreneurship & Libraries Conference. "About the ELC." Accessed at https://entrelib.org/about-the-elc/.
19. BRASS: RUSA's Business Reference and Services Section. "Business Reference Essentials." Accessed at https://brass.libguides.com/BusinessReference
20. NACE. "Class of 2022 Employment Rate Matched Pre-Pandemic Level." Accessed at https://www.naceweb.org/about-us/press/class-of-2022-employment-rate-matched-pre-pandemic-level.
21. CareerOneStop. "Looking for a Job? Many Employers Are Hiring." Accessed at https://www.careeronestop.org/EmploymentRecovery/FindAJobNow/whos-hiring.aspx

22. National Skills Coalition. "About NSC." Accessed at https://nationalskillscoalition.org/about/
23. National Skills Coalition. "Libraries and Workforce Development: Connecting the Dots between Your Patrons and Public Policy [Video file]." March 30, 2021. Accessed at https://www.youtube.com/watch?v=NgpQdKYQbqA
24. Workforce Monitor: Explanatory Articles on Workforce Development. "About Workforce Monitor." Accessed at https://wfmonitor.com/about/
25. Cruse, L. R., J. Stiddard, R. Taylor, and J. LaPrad. "The Non-degree Credential Quality Imperative. Workforce Monitor: Explanatory Articles on Workforce Development." October 20, 2023. Accessed at https://wfmonitor.com/2023/10/20/ndcquality/ (Originally published on July 19, 2023, by the National Skills Coalition)
26. Measures that Matter. "About MtM." Accessed at https://measuresthatmatter.net/about/.
27. Pothier, W., and P. Condon. "Cultivating a Data Literate Workforce: Considerations for Librarians." *Portal: Libraries and the Academy*, vol. twenty-three, no. four (2023): 628.
28. Ibid., 634.
29. Birdeye. "14 Tools and 7 Strategies to Use AI for Small Businesses." Accessed at https://birdeye.com/blog/ai-for-small-businesses/#h-14-ai-tools-to-scale-up-your-small-business.
30. SLAAIT. "Information." Accessed at https://circl.community/index.php/slaait-home/.
31. Bloomberg Law. "Insights." Accessed at https://pro.bloomberglaw.com/brief/state-privacy-legislation-tracker/.
32. Pluralsight. "All about ChatGPT's First Data Breach, and How It Happened." June 01, 2023. Accessed at https://www.pluralsight.com/blog/security-professional/chatgpt-data-breach.
33. American Library Association. "ALA Releases New Libraries Build Business Playbook to Encourage Small Business Development in Public Libraries." *Tue*, January 2, 2022. Accessed at https://www.ala.org/news/press-releases/2022/02/ala-releases-new-libraries-build-business-playbook-encourage-small-business.
34. American Library Association. Public Library Association. "Public Library Staff and Diversity Report: Results from the 2021 PLA Annual Survey." Accessed at https://www.ala.org/pla/sites/ala.org.pla/files/content/data/PLA_Staff_Survey_Report_2022.pdf.
35. Reference and User Services Association (RUSA). "Academic BRASS Volume eighteen, No. 2." Accessed at https://www.ala.org/rusa/sections/brass/publications/academicbrass/2023/18-2.
36. Liu, G. "Business Librarians' Roles in Supporting AACSB Accreditation: A Discussion about the Potentials." *Academic BRASS*, vol. 16, no. 2 (Fall 2021). Accessed at https://www.ala.org/rusa/sites/ala.org.rusa/files/content/sections/brass/Publications/Acad_BRASS/2021_fall_liu.pdf
37. Reference and User Services Association (RUSA). "Guidelines for Business Information Responses." Accessed at https://www.ala.org/rusa/resources/guidelines/business.
38. Public Libraries Online. Podcast: "FYI 63—Workforce Development—Clark—Ruppert" [Audio podcast episode]. Accessed at https://soundcloud.com/publiclibrariesonline/pla-fyi-podcast-63-workforce-development-clark-ruppert.

39. Library Leadership Podcast. "Episode 133: The Library's Role in Economic Development with Diane Luccy and Julie Brophy" [Audio podcast episode]. July 31, 2023. Accessed at https://libraryleadershippodcast.com/133-the-librarys-role-in-economic-development-with-diane-luccy-and-julie-brophy/.
40. Workforce Waves. "E22: How Libraries Help Job Seekers and Employers" [Audio podcast episode]. Accessed at https://workforcewaves.libsyn.com/e22-how-libraries-help-job-seekers-and-employers.
41. Aspen Ideas. "Work and Life Advice for the Nonlinear Path" [Audio podcast episode]. Accessed at https://www.aspenideas.org/podcasts/work-and-life-advice-for-the-nonlinear-path.
42. Aspen Ideas. "Investing in Shared American Prosperity" [Audio podcast episode]. Accessed at https://www.aspenideas.org/podcasts/investing-in-shared-american-prosperity.

5

Vignettes and Scenarios

This chapter covers the following:

- Vignettes and common scenarios where career services librarians may support a job seeker
- Strategies in addressing such common scenarios

There are many questions that a career services librarian or workforce librarian may encounter. Here, we offer some common requests and scenarios that you may get and ways to address these questions from community members regardless of library types. These requests came from our experiences as public librarians, business librarians, career coaches, and more. We responded to these questions based on our experiences and expertise in resources and referrals. Generative AI tools were not used to answer these prompts. Although if you used them, the results and suggestions might be different.

QUESTIONS AND SCENARIOS

Scenario 1: How would you suggest someone just a couple years out of school start building a career network? I am not sure who to talk to or what about.
Response: It depends on what the patron is interested in networking in. Are they into finance, healthcare work, education, or something else? Once you find out, you can recommend local groups such as the Chamber of Commerce or professional associations for them to join and be more involved (see chapter 1). Networking means making time to get to know people and connecting. We do not recommend "cold" connecting or calling people in the industry via LinkedIn because it does not build the relationship that supports the patron.

Take the time to read professional literature in the field, which you can find in the databases or on websites and make an effort to connect in networking events and follow up on LinkedIn. Eventually, you may want to volunteer to host, to participate, or connect others too. By building a network gradually and making your name involved visibly, it will help expand your opportunities to enhance your profile. You want to also keep your digital profiles open such as LinkedIn and social media accounts, in a reputable and professional manner. It takes time and you can also participate in library workshops on networking if it is being offered too.

Scenario 2: A recent graduate who might be trying to get a job outside of the field they are in, what advice do you have?
Response: Similar to the first scenario: you will want to know what they are trying to move to and what they majored in and work experiences they currently have. If they are trying to make a complete change in a field, consider networking opportunities to expand referrals and informational interviews and to build upon transferable skills in one's resume and cover letter.

Depending on the type of position and industry that they are interested in, they will need to make connections with professionals in those industries and learn more about the work that is applicable to their skill sets. They may want to read industry and company news to stay informed about the areas they are interested in. Perhaps, they may need to consider continuing education and pursue more training in the specific area of interest. This may require loans and other financial support, which you may be able to identify appropriate graduate programs and scholarships through foundations such as Candid Learning [https://learning.candid.org/] or commercial sites such as Fastweb: Scholarships [http://www.fastweb.com].

Scenario 3: Do you have recommendations for transitioning from unpaid or paid internship/part-time/temporary position to a full-time position?
Response: When you have an internship (paid or unpaid), it is an opportunity to network and learn from colleagues as much as you can. Unfortunately, internships are temporary and it may also be inequitable to be in an unpaid internship but there are ways to maximize one's potential there. Some internships may actually turn into permanent employment. This is dependent on the employer's skill needs, budget, and openings, and your own experiences and skills. You would be an internal candidate and may need to go through the process like an external candidate. Internal candidates may have advantages and disadvantages but you should prepare the interview process as if you are new and the best candidate for the position. For external opportunities, it is obvious to highlight relevant skills, projects, and experiences to these positions but what might be helpful is if you know someone from those companies and may be able to learn more about the organization or get a referral/recommendation.

Part-time/temporary work is not for everyone and can be stressful for those seeking full-time work, which often comes with benefits and other perks.

A part-time job could turn into a full-time job if you demonstrate value to the organization by going above and beyond your work duty, but that is to say to not overcommit to the organization but rather do your job very well and be engaged and informed. Networking internally should be treated like you are networking externally, getting to know folks and collaborating on projects and being supportive and helpful. Part-time positions may become full-time positions but you may also need to interview for them.

Scenario 4: Do you have any advice for seasoned or long time workers? I am concerned about my age. I see it as many years of professional and life experience with a lot to contribute, but I do not know if recruiters are looking for younger candidates.
Response: Highlighting your wealth of work experiences and skills can be your advantage. If you have worked in numerous places, it demonstrates your flexibility and ability to grow and learn new working environments quickly. Ageism is real and unfortunately exists as an implicit and explicit bias. We hope that more human resources are aware of such concerns and address them within the organization through training and conversation with employees. It depends on your interest in such a position. For example, if you are looking for a new type of work, it is challenging to always start a second or third career but it is not impossible. It requires networking, and deep curiosity, passion, and examples of collaboration and proactiveness.

Transferable skills are definitely critical to highlight to recruiters in your resume/cover letter and in your interviews. If the position requires technology skills that you may lack, consider enrolling in a library workshop or learning program that offers such training. Fill the gaps as much as possible so you are confident in talking about them and you should be networking with industry leaders to learn more and to demonstrate your curiosity.

Scenario 5: I am leaning toward online school for financial reasons but am worried about opportunities to get experience in the field if I am working full-time in my current job and going to school. Would a degree and volunteer experience be enough to get a new job?
Response: Yes and no. It depends on the position. Some positions within specific industries are high in demand if you check the U.S. Bureau of Labor Statistics [https://www.bls.gov/]. You may want to prepare your skills within the degree to ensure that you are able to do the position. Volunteering can expand your experience, even if it is not related to your first job/position; it can demonstrate your soft skills and transferable skills. An online program can be difficult to talk about collaborative or team work, which many industries are seeking people to have these experiences. You can see it listed by job title in the Occupational Information Network [https://www.onetonline.org/find/descriptor/result/4.C.1.b.1.e]. Many positions require this skill to be important

in the role. Group projects and volunteer work either within a professional association or via internship that involves collaboration can expand your experiences and skills. Your current position also helps you to explain transferable skills and make connections to your next job.

Scenario 6: How do you tactfully explain a gap in employment that is due to leaving a toxic workplace?
Response: This one is very unfortunate and common for most people experiencing a toxic workplace. A toxic workplace can be described as a workplace that challenges the psychological, emotional, mental and physical well-being of the worker. It can be caused by a number of factors including coworkers, supervisors, clients, workload, inflexibility, demand of the job/position, and so forth. Depending on your gap, did you volunteer or take up online learning programs? That might be a way to explain how you kept professionally occupied with learning and growth.

If they ask you directly during the interview, you could say that you wanted new challenges and opportunities to grow. Always speak positively about your former workplace and explain what you've learned and what you are seeking to learn in this potential new role. Always prepare a response in case they ask you that.

Scenario 7: You have a patron who is interested in changing careers from restaurant industry to art education. What would you recommend?
Response: We might recommend exploring art education programs through online certification or learning such as Coursera, Udacity, and Future Learn before investing into a formal academic program. These online programs might be available in your library. It might be an expensive process if you went directly for an academic program. From there, if they feel convinced in pursuing this career, they should explore art education programs in colleges; they may consider joining the National Art Education Association [https://www.arteducators.org/] to network and identify mentors and hold informational interviews to learn more about job opportunities and expectations. You may want to explore how to become an art teacher through teacher credentialing programs based on your state's requirements. A formal art education program may be associated with this process and you may need to network to identify work opportunities. Good luck!

Scenario 8: A patron is coming to seek job support. They do not have an email address to start off with. What do you suggest?
Response: Applying for a job for this patron may require a multi-step process. First, you should gather information about the patron and their experiences with computers. You may want to ask the patron if they are comfortable using the computer. It is likely that they may not be and you may offer computer

classes that your library may be offering. If not, you could support the user by showing basics and help sign them up for online classes in using computers. You can direct them to a computer station in the library. If you have handouts, you may want to print them out for the patron to follow along. For setting up an email account, you can walk them through setting up an email through Yahoo, Gmail, or other email service provider. You will need to ask them if they have a cover letter or resume. If they do not, offer a handout on how to set up a resume in a word document. Searching for jobs online and then applying for these jobs are other crucial steps that take time for the patron to get to. It would not be a one day process but an ongoing process. If your library has volunteers, they may also be able to provide support for patrons with limited computer skills.

Scenario 9: A patron seeking career coaching is interested in starting their own small business in selling their own crafts. How should they proceed?
Response: It may be easy to share on etsy or some kind of store but there are tons of crafts and your patron may not be able to sell effectively. They may want to look at different types of information before starting their own crafts. For example, they may want to check the business databases for statistics about the craft industry. What does the market research data or reports say about market size or consumers? Does this patron use social media? What are their experiences in using social media to promote their small business? The patron will need to explore the Small Business Administration website, market research, website domain, and social media channels, and how they plan to develop and market their crafts for sale.

Scenario 10: A student wants to start their own startup focusing on cryptocurrency consultation, specifically in New York. What should they look into?
Response: If students want to start their own startup business, you may refer them to SCORE for startup advice and TechCrunch on technology news. If you are an academic librarian, be sure to note that your database licenses are restricted to academic research. If this was for a research project for a class, they may want to find out the companies that deal with cryptocurrency by exploring databases like PrivCo, which might detail information about private firms and companies regarding investors and financial information. Your library will need to have a subscription to PrivCo. Checking the newspaper, news, and media databases can also provide information on companies managing cryptocurrency and some of their updates and trends coming up.

CHAPTER SUMMARY

This chapter highlights select questions and scenarios and how to address them. It is not comprehensive but should provide samples to think about and to prepare your work going forward. There may be other questions or inquiries that may happen in your information or reference services where you or your colleagues may encounter such questions that are worth collecting so you and your colleagues can know how to prepare to respond to these questions and offer timely support.

Appendix A

SURVEY

Name (Optional): _____

Email Address (Optional): _____

Date: _____

Name of Library Program Attended: _____

1. Why did you attend today's event/session?

2. How did you hear about today's event/session ?

3. What did you get out of today's event/session?

4. What would you like to know or learn more regarding today's event/session?

5. If you enjoyed the session, would you refer others to the program? Y/N

6. How does the library meet your needs?

7. If we wanted to reach out to you to learn more about your experiences, could you please leave your email address: _____ and a member of the library team will reach out for additional comments.

Appendix B

INTERVIEWS/FOCUS GROUPS

Name of Focus Group Interviewer: _____

Date: _____

1. Why did you attend today's event/session?

2. How did you hear about today's event/session?

3. What did you get out of today's event/session?

4. What would you like to know or learn more regarding today's event/session?

5. If you enjoyed the session, would you refer others to the program? Y/N

6. What would you suggest for the library to consider related to career development support?

7. How does the library meet your needs?

8. If we wanted to reach out to you to learn more about your experiences, could you please leave your email address: _____ and a member of the library team will reach out for additional comments.

Appendix C

PRACTICE QUESTIONS IN INTERVIEWS

Questions that might be commonly asked during an interview (please note: some questions are scenario or behavior based to assess how an applicant handles previous challenges):

- Tell us why you are interested in this position?
- Tell us about your strengths and weaknesses?
- Can you give us an example where you worked in a team?
- Where do you want to be in five years?
- Tell us about a time when you failed and what lessons did you learn from this experience?
- Can you tell us a time when you started an initiative?
- Tell us a time when you went above and beyond your job duty.
- Give us an example when you had to deal with a conflict.
- How do you handle a situation when you have to meet multiple deadlines?
- How would you handle a difficult client or customer?

Questions interviewees should consider asking:

- What do you hope this hire will accomplish six months from now?
- How would you describe the administrative and fiscal health of your organization?
- Tell me about your company's position on [value] (e.g., data privacy, intellectual freedom, censorship, climate change, state legislation, diversity, equity, and inclusion . . .)
- How does your team handle coverage when someone goes on vacation?
- What have people in similar roles gone on to do?
- What is your outlook on any imminent mergers or acquisitions?
- What are team norms when it comes to computing hardware/peripherals?

- What applications do you use for email, communication, productivity, or other important functions?
- What does your performance evaluation process look like?
- How do you communicate with your direct reports, and what's the typical frequency/duration of 1:1 meetings?
- [For on-site working locations, esp. in older buildings] How is the condition/health of the facility? Any HVAC, plumbing, or other issues I should be aware of?

Appendix D

RESUME FORMATTING

This appendix document can be used to share with a job seeker as an example. There are plenty online that one can find to see. A resume is generally one page long but 1.5-2 pages might work if you have extensive work experience. Remember to keep fonts consistent, past work experiences in the past tense, and keep all activities in bullet points with quantifiers. The sample below is to give you an example of what one type of resume can look like.

Jamie Lee [Insert name]
Address and Email Address and Phone Number [Keep this information at the top]

WORK HISTORY

Senior Administrative Associate, January 5, 2017-Present
Myers and Son Firm, Dallas, TX

- Coordinate, organize, and schedule over 50+ clients' appointments weekly to meet with senior consultant partners.
- Collaborate with senior partners to establish and enforce policies of record keeping, and updating, and reviewing files for safekeeping and for confidentiality.
- Maintain files of over 100+ clients and train 5+ new associates on managing files.
- Serve as primary point contact for over 20+ company events with draws in over 1,000+ customers for each event.

Research Associate, March 20, 2015-December 1, 2027
University of Higher Education, San Antonio, TX

- Drafted and reviewed research and annual budgets for Dr. Jackie Klein through a spreadsheet; budgets ranged from $1.5 to 2 million.
- Entered data and generated monthly reports on research progress.
- Attended biweekly meetings and took minutes and followed up on next steps for each research teams.

SKILLS

- Attention to details such as budget sheets and minutes
- Event planning and scheduling
- Proficient in MS Suite and Google products
- Strong public speaking skills

EDUCATION

Bachelor of Arts: Sociology, December 2014
University of Higher Education, San Antonio, TX

Appendix E

ASSESSMENT MEETING WITH A JOB SEEKER

Date: ___ / ___ / ___   Time: _____

Your Name (Job Seeker's): _____

Counselor's Name: _____

- What brings you in today for career services?
- What do you hope to accomplish in this session?

_____
_____
_____

Your Notes:

_____
_____
_____

Next Action Steps:
After this meeting with a career counselor, I want to complete the following steps in the next twenty-four to forty-eight hours.

- _____

- _____

Index

academic libraries, ix, x, 1, 3, 17, 23, 26, 33, 41, 44, 46, 51, 54, 57, 59, 60, 62-65, 73-75, 77, 80, 93, 97, 98, 103, 115, 121
adult learning theories, 115-16, 127
advertisement, 10, 22, 24, 36
advocacy, xi, 14-15, 34, 70, 85, 89, 91-93, 95, 97-104, 110-11, 118, 121, 124, 125
agriculture, 51
The American Library Association (ALA), 5, 12, 38, 71, 89, 91, 102, 121, 125
artificial intelligence (AI), ix, x, 23, 49-50, 77, 79-81, 85, 89-91, 104, 123
arts, 41-42
The Aspen Institute, 126-27
assessment, 126-27
Association of College and Research Libraries (ACRL), 6, 121
Association to Advance Collegiate Schools of Business (AACSB International), 98, 125

business cards, 9, 11
business field, 14, 22, 26, 45-49
business owners, 12, 14, 16, 34, 35, 65, 69-72, 89, 95, 101, 103-4, 119, 121, 124
Business Reference and Services Section (BRASS), 71, 74, 98, 103, 121, 124, 125

calendar management software, 21
career coach, 3, 22, 29-33, 90, 106, 116, 118
career fair, 3-4
career information literacy, 39-40
Career One Stop, 49, 54, 61, 96, 118, 121
Career Talk Series, 4-5
certification, 59, 76, 77, 118, 134
ChatGPT, 23, 27, 49-51, 85, 90. *See also* artificial intelligence
climate, 6, 48, 100
coaching. *See* career coach
collection development, 17-19
community college, 62, 69, 75, 76, 103, 104, 122
company research, 45-47
computer basics, 18
consultations, 3, 14-17
cover letter, ix, 3-4, 14, 18, 49-50, 78, 90
COVID-19, ix-x, 2, 16, 20, 29, 34, 36, 38, 84, 124
curriculum vitae (CV), 1-3

data literacy, 120, 123
digital badge, 11-12, 73-74
digital literacy, 16, 23, 87, 104, 108-9, 120
diversity, 97, 108, 124
Dressing for Success, 9

economics, 45-46
education, 52-53

147

embedded librarianship, 39, 41, 55, 59–61
e-newsletter, 9–10
engineering, 5, 51–52
entrepreneurship, 7, 14, 15, 22, 34, 65, 69–72, 75, 89, 92–95, 98, 102, 108, 119–21, 124, 125
equity, 91, 102, 108, 124
expungement clinic, 14–15, 67–68

Facebook, 10, 18
finance, 46, 52, 55, 74
first year students, 53–56
flyer, 10, 26, 95, 105, 117
focus group, 13, 139
future career paths, x, xi, 1–2, 48–49, 87–90, 93, 122, 124

graduate school, 2–3, 19, 56–57

headshot, 6–7
health sciences, 44–45
higher education, 1, 3, 62–64, 95–98, 123
high impact practices, 97
humanities, 41–42
The Human Library, 6

immigrants, 11–12, 16, 66–67
Immigration Consultation Day, 16
inclusion, 108–9
industry research, 45–48, 56
information literacy, 11, 39–45, 98
Instagram, 10, 18
internship, 3–4, 19, 30, 54, 97, 107, 125, 132, 134
interview, viii, ix, 1, 4–9, 11, 13–14, 19, 23, 79, 90, 110, 125, 139, 141

job advertisement. See advertisement
job searching, 7, 13, 18, 49–50, 138
job training, 89, 116–19, 121, 123–26
job trends. See future career paths

legal support, 15–16
lesson plan, 15–16
liaison, 22, 27, 31–32, 59–60, 64, 73, 88
Libraries Build Business, 12, 69, 71, 93–95, 98, 102–5
library advocacy. See advocacy
LinkedIn, 10–11, 17, 18, 29, 32, 131
loud quitting, ix

makerspace, 9, 92, 104
mathematics, 51–52
multilingual support, 16, 53, 72

National Association of Colleges and Employers (NACE), 121
National Skills Coalition (NSC), 122
networking, 18, 23, 29, 33, 106, 131, 133
news media, 3–4, 10–11, 92

open access, 42–46, 49, 53

pandemic. See COVID-19
partnerships, x, 3–4, 6, 15, 17, 19, 20, 22–28, 30–34, 39, 62–66, 68–70, 72, 102, 117, 123
people with disabilities, 3, 28, 31, 35, 44, 69–70
podcast, 10–11, 15–16, 125–27
professional associations, 5, 61, 64, 65, 88, 95, 102, 118, 124–27
professional development, 23, 27–28, 106, 109, 110, 115, 116, 118, 127
project management, 18
public libraries, ix–x, xi, 6, 11, 15, 17, 19, 20, 22, 23, 66–67, 102, 104, 121–24, 128–29
Public Library association (PLA), x, xii, 6, 15, 63, 82, 124–25

quiet quitting, ix

rage quitting, ix
reentry/transition, 14-15, 25, 31, 67-69, 92, 120
Reference and User Services Association (RUSA), 74, 112, 121, 124, 128
referral, 14, 60, 66, 69, 70, 116-17, 126
refugees, 66-67
research, x, xi, 3-6, 39-59, 76, 77, 80, 88, 90, 96-98, 103, 106, 107, 109-10, 124-25, 135
resume, ix, 1-4, 6, 14, 18, 22, 23, 26, 28-33, 49, 54, 65, 74, 76, 81, 106, 118, 143
rural, 64-65, 99-101, 124

sciences, 51-52
skill building, 6, 11, 64, 88, 93, 116
social media, 6, 10, 18, 24, 35, 66, 72, 92, 95, 132
social sciences, 43-44
state libraries, 99-105, 124
suburban, 64, 100, 123
survey, x, xii, 2, 4, 6, 13, 24, 33, 90, 92, 121, 124, 137
sustainability, 88-89

technical career, 57-58, 96, 117
technology, 4, 6, 8-9, 14, 20-22, 33, 60, 62, 68, 86-87, 89-90, 97, 101, 104, 106, 108, 124
teenagers, ix, xi, xii, 4, 22

TikTok, 10, 18
trade associations, 5, 58, 61, 88, 117

unemployment, 14, 22, 49, 68, 70, 86, 89, 128
unemployment benefit, 14
unhoused, 65-66
United States Chamber of Commerce, 5, 61, 70, 72, 84, 86, 92, 110, 131
urban, vii, 33, 64, 65, 100, 123
Urban Libraries Council (ULC), 49, 71-72, 94

veterans, 62, 65, 96, 122
virtual programming, ix, x, 4, 6, 8, 20, 49, 95-96, 98, 100, 120
vocational career, 19, 55, 57-58, 69, 98, 117

website, 10, 18, 49-50
women, 35, 72, 110
Workforce Monitor (WFM), 122
WorkingNation, 122
workshops, 1-4, 6-9, 14-15, 18-19, 29-30, 32, 41-59
work systems, 3

X, 10, 18

young adults. *See* teenagers

Zoom. *See* virtual programming

About the Authors

Arpine Eloyan is a Community Library Manager in Los Angeles County Library. She has previously worked in Glendale Public Library in various roles. Native speaker of Armenian, Arpine is an experienced librarian with many years working in public libraries such as collection maintenance, community, and social services engagement, especially with the Armenian community. Arpine earned her MLIS from University of North Texas and BA in Theater from UC Riverside.

Michael R. Oppenheim has been Business Research and Collections Librarian in the Rosenfeld Management Library, UCLA Anderson Graduate School of Management, since 1997. Prior to working at UCLA, he was a government information and reference librarian at California State University, Los Angeles, and the federal documents depository librarian at Whittier College. He is active in the American Library Association (ALA) and has held various offices in its Business Reference and Services Section (BRASS) and the Government Documents Roundtable (GODORT), as well as in the California Library Association, the Business and Finance Division of the Special Libraries Association, and California Academic and Research Libraries (CARL). With Eric Forte (OCLC), he coedited *The Basic Business Library: Core Resources and Services*, 5th edition (2012), and with Wendy Diamond (California State University-Chico, retired) he is coauthor of *Marketing Information: A Strategic Guide for Business and Finance Libraries* (2004). He is the 2013 recipient of the ALA/RUSA/BRASS Award for "Excellence in Business Librarianship."

Raymond Pun is the Academic and Research Librarian at the Alder Graduate School of Education, where he is responsible for all library services/programs. He has served as a career coach for the New York Public Library's Career Center and has experiences as a business librarian supporting entrepreneurship programs. He has also published and presented on library partnerships with career centers. In addition, he is a member of ALA Policy Corps focusing on policy issues such as workforce development in libraries. In his past experiences, he has partnered with Student Affairs, Career Development Center, Writing Center, and other departments to create student engagement programs. Pun served as President of the Asian/Pacific American Librarians Association (APALA) and the Chinese American Librarians Association (CALA).

www.ingramcontent.com/pod-product-compliance
Lightning Source LLC
Chambersburg PA
CBHW070333230426
43663CB00011B/2302